The World Class Rainmaker:
Raising the Bar in Your Law Practice

The World Class Rainmaker:
Raising the Bar in Your Law Practice

Robin M. Hensley
and
Lance J. LoRusso, Esq.

Alpharetta, Georgia

ISBN: 978-1-61005-255-9

Library of Congress Control Number: 2012917926

Printed in the United States of America

∞This paper meets the requirements of ANSI/NISO Z39.48-1992 (Permanence of Paper)

Table of Contents

A MESSAGE FROM ROBIN

While rainmaking is probably one of many good reasons you moved into a leadership role within your firm, the more distant you are from the day-to-day requirements for rainmaking, the more inevitable is the erosion of those skills. A world class rainmaking practice *is* within your reach. The following pages will show you how to change what must be changed to achieve that goal.

I know what it takes to become a world class rainmaker. I learned this as a business development coach seeing more than forty individual attorneys every week who fly into Atlanta from over twenty-seven cities to learn how to be more efficient and make more rain in less time with less effort. I understand the demands upon you working, as I have done, in marketing and business development for two law firms. I began my career learning how to make my own rain as a CPA. I know what a struggle it is to meet the demands of managing a professional practice and still find time to develop new business, manage administrative details, and have something left over for a personal life.

The information you will find here comes from my own search for systems and resources to help me be more effective and successful at managing both the business and personal side of my life. I know they will work for you, as they do for my clients and me, when you put them into practice. Often it is the implementation that is the trick. Seek out a mentor, partner, friend, or coach to help you stay on track. You need it *and* you deserve it!

All the best,

Robin Hensley
The Business Development Coach for World Class Rainmakers
President, Raising the Bar
www.raisingthebar.com

A MESSAGE FROM LANCE

As a lawyer, I will address potential legal or ethical issues that may come to mind as you read *The World Class Rainmaker: Raising the Bar in Your Law Practice.* These include topics such as delegating tasks, advertising, accepting new clients, referring clients, and discharging clients. I will explore how Robin's recommendations should be handled to comply with the Rules of Professional Conduct as listed by the Georgia Bar Association. We will also look at how Robin's methodology will help you maintain compliance with those standards. After all, professional responsibility is all about competence, loyalty to the client, and service to the profession.

I will also discuss the role of the rainmaker as a mentor. Rainmaking is focused upon building a practice that helps clients accomplish their goals and solve their problems. Lawyers learn early that proper attention to client matters requires a division of labor to ensure professional quality in the representation. While this is normally the subject of mentoring sessions between senior attorneys and their associates, the mentor must surpass these goals. Every mentoring lawyer must impart onto young lawyers the importance and skills of rainmaking. We all stand taller when we help others stand on their own. We owe this to the associates who look to us for guidance in every other area of the practice of law. It is not enough to hand them work and praise them for a job well done. A true mentor prepares their charges for their professional future, not the next billing cycle. Only through teaching the importance of rainmaking and imparting the skills to build a law practice will lawyers take their associates to the next level and prepare them for a successful career. There is an ancillary benefit to training a new cadre of rainmakers in your firm; the new rain they make will make your garden prosper as well.

In this book, you will learn how to increase your efficiency so that you can better serve your clients. If you are an old hand at marketing and building your practice, you will find new concepts that will help you take your practice to the next level. If you are new to rainmaking, dive in. The water is refreshing!

Best practice,

Lance LoRusso
Principal Attorney and Owner
LoRusso Law Firm
www.lorussolawfirm.com

A FEW WORDS ABOUT ETHICS AND RAISING THE BAR FROM LANCE

As you begin to incorporate the principles in this book and your mind begins to generate ideas of marketing and wooing clients, a part of your brain may spring back to your law school classes on professional responsibility. You begin to remember the public announcements about lawyers who became entangled with the Bar Association over issues like advertising, client solicitation, and myriad potential conflicts that can arise while building your business.

Not to worry. In each section of this book, I will explore scenarios that may arise and how the Georgia Rules of Professional Conduct apply. Remember, the *Georgia Supreme Court adopted new standards and ethical guidelines effective January 1, 2001. The new standards more closely match the national guidelines. You may view these standards and ethical guidelines at www.gabar.org. Make sure that you refer to the newest guidelines when evaluating your activities.*

Keep in mind, you can *always* seek ethical input from the Georgia Bar. The Bar provides a helpline for attorneys who do not have anyone to consult on such matters or who seek guidance without the intervention of other lawyers in their firm.

You can reach the Ethics Helpline at 800-682-9806 or via email through the link at www.gabar.org under the link for "Ethics." Your inquiry will be directed to the assistant general counsel or grievance counsel. They will respond in writing or by phone call. Upon call back, counsel will clarify the issue and advise you on the appropriate course of action by reference to the rules, ethical standards or advisory opinions.

Bar Rule 4-403(g) requires the Office of the General Counsel to treat as confidential the name of a lawyer requesting an informal advisory opinion. This confidential system works. I know, because I have called the Ethics Helpline on more than one occasion. The assistant general counsel and grievance counsel have a great deal of unique experience with the rules governing the practice of law. Do not hesitate to call upon them to seek the benefit of their experience.

PART ONE:

TAKE TIME TO PLAN

1

SETTING GOALS FOR YOUR LAW PRACTICE...AND YOUR LIFE

Planning is bringing the future into the present
so you can do something about it.
– Alan Lakein

Is goal setting a regular part of your routine? Have you made it a part of your firm's practice? Is every member of your team setting goals and working to achieve them? If you want to reinvigorate your firm's business development efforts and bring your own skills back to world class status, then goal setting is the first step.

Let's start with *your* goals. Have you ever dreamed of climbing Mt. Everest? Maybe you just wish you could get your to-do list under control; or even find the time to actually think about what you want to accomplish. We all have goals—for work, home, family, and for the future. There is no time like *right now* to make a plan that will help you achieve those long-term goals for the next twelve months.

In this chapter, we talk about how to set realistic, meaningful goals for your law practice, your firm and your life. I'll give you some ideas for setting aside time to plan and focusing on what is most important. I'll also ask you ten simple questions that could dramatically change your results, as they did for me in my coaching practice when I first tried the method I will share with you.

First, let's look at this whole goal-setting thing. Do goals really work? Research shows that setting goals takes people to new heights, both personally and professionally. In fact, in a study conducted among business school grads ten or more years after getting their MBA, those with some sense of their goals were earning three times more than those without goals, and those with written goals earned ten times more than those with no goals at all. A compelling argument for setting goals, wouldn't you say? Learning how to set and achieve goals has dramatically changed my own results, and that simple process is the foundation for the success my world class rainmaker clients achieve as well; so I know what a difference it can make for you. Let's get started.

In my experience, taking the time to set your goals may be the biggest obstacle of all. Perhaps you tried to take an hour or so out of your day at the first of the year for goal setting. That day you ended up going to a breakfast meeting, then moved on to a meeting with a client, had lunch with your partners or the rest of your team, had a difficult conversation with one of your associates, stopped by a client's open house, fought traffic and dodged roadwork all the way home. Whew! Then your kids met you at the door, ready to play. Now you are exhausted, without having much left for planning the next year of your life. You may even resent that you always seem to be running from one meeting to the next —that you never get to sit back and reflect on what is most important right now, much less for the next twelve months. But that failure to plan, to keep the promises you make to yourself, has bigger consequences. Over time, it erodes your confidence in your ability to make the changes that will produce the results you want. As Jinny Ditzler describes in her book, *YOUR BEST YEAR YET*, "We come to believe that we're not capable of making the changes that matter, and therefore we stop setting goals and planning ahead in any meaningful way. And the life we really want for ourselves drifts out of reach." OUCH! That's exactly the situation I found myself in a few years ago.

An online search will turn up literally hundreds of goal-setting programs, methods and techniques, but I found that Jinny Ditzler's *BEST YEAR YET* program, with its straightforward how-to goal-setting strategy, has been the most useful and effective for me and the people with whom I work. What started as Jinny's own personal goal-setting system has gone on to become a standard for individuals, corporations and professional practices worldwide. I think it is the sheer simplicity of it that makes it so effective.

BYY's process starts with a one-time annual three-hour commitment you make to yourself to answer just ten simple questions. Of course, you will have to make and keep that commitment to yourself for Jinny's system to work. I find that carving out three hours on a Saturday morning, with a definite purpose in mind, makes the commitment pill go down a lot easier. Choose a day and time that works for you, perhaps incorporating it into something you already want to do, like taking a break at your local bookstore, library, or café. Next, you'll be asking yourself ten questions.

The first four questions ask you to look back at last year. When you think about last year:

- **What did you accomplish?**
- **What were your biggest disappointments?**
- **What did you learn?**
- **How do you limit yourself, and how can you stop?**

Did one or more of those strike a nerve?

The next four questions ask you to take a look at yourself in terms of what is most important to you in the various roles you play in life, based on your personal values. We all have values that guide us. Some examples of values could be integrity, family, harmony, drive, or accomplishment. When you think about what is important to you:

- **What are *your* personal values?**

We all play many roles. Looking at those roles is a valuable way of integrating all the areas of your life, while placing yourself and your personal values at the center. Some examples of roles you might play are attorney, parent, litigator, advocate, husband, wife, founding partner, son, daughter, subordinate, Little League coach, volunteer, and so forth. Take a look at yourself:

- **What roles do *you* play in your life?**
- **List all the roles you play and then narrow that list down to a maximum of eight.**
- **Write out no more than three goals for each of those roles.**

Now drill down even further:

- **Which role is your major focus for the next twelve months?**

Now let's move into goal-setting:

- **What are your goals for this year?**
- **Write down all that you want to achieve this year, according to each role you play.**

Drilling down to what is most important will help you stay focused:

- **What are your top ten overall goals for this year?** Make sure to consider all of your roles.

The next step is not a question, but an exercise. Once you have your ten goals selected, imagine yourself in a year's time having achieved each of them:

- **How will you feel?** *How thrilled will you be with what you have accomplished?*

But you're not finished yet. The final step in the goal-setting process is the *reality check*. Ask yourself:

- **Is meeting each of my goals possible?**
- **Can I really do it?**

Check your list again to be sure that each role you play has at least one goal. This will ensure that your plan leads you to a more balanced life and lifestyle. Finally, the kicker question:

- **How can you make sure you achieve your goals?**

No need to think about that now. That's what we'll be talking about in Chapter Two.

Let's wrap up this section:

1. **People who set goals achieve more than those who don't.**
2. **Written goals with an action plan produce the best results.**
3. **Taking time to plan is often the biggest challenge.**

4. **The rewards for goal setting go far beyond the goals themselves.** You will feel more confident and capable when you take the time to plan.

5. **Choose a goal-setting system that works for you.** My favorite is BEST YEAR YET. You can learn more about it online at bestyearyet.com.

6. **As important as setting goals is, planning how you will achieve them is what drives results.** We'll talk about that in the next chapter.

LEGAL & ETHICAL CONSIDERATIONS

Robin appropriately starts out the book with some practical considerations about how to make your practice and your life more rewarding and fulfilling. This is a reminder for all of us in the legal profession. As you know, it is often difficult to follow Robin's advice during days filled with deadlines. However, while Robin talks about goals in the balance of your life, you would benefit from written goals in the balance of your practice as well.

For example, lawyers often register for continuing legal education (CLE) classes based upon three criteria. Is this class or conference convenient? Are we short on hours this year and will this class satisfy the requirements? Is this the conference that my friends attend every year? If we change this analysis, and every lawyer goes through this decision-making process every year, we find that our professional goals and rainmaking goals advance toward a new goal line.

Let's change the CLE selection process starting right now! Take thirty minutes at the end of each quarter and decide what area of law you would like to explore. That's right. I said "like" not "must." If you have been practicing for a few years, it is easy to get stale or burned out on the area of law you work in each day. How many of you have been to a CLE and realized you knew more than the instructors or had more experience in those areas? Perhaps it is time to look elsewhere! If you intend to take time to engage in this type of analysis, put it on your calendar! This is just as important as a client matter.

Take the time to speak with your associates about their CLE plans and goals. You may find that one of your associates in your transactional practice has a desire to learn about helping families adapt to ailing and disabled relatives. Encouraging that employee to take eight CLE hours may lead to a new resource for your clients or a new practice area for your firm. The associate with an undergraduate degree in finance may benefit from a CLE on forensic accounting instead of the usual conference on restrictive covenants. Encourage your associates to explore new areas of the law while they are learning.

Speaking of rainmaking, if you attend the same conference every year, see the same people at the conference and have the same client list every year when you see them, perhaps there is a pattern here! Switch things up! Attend a conference in a new area of law or with a new organization. Or at least sit with a different group of people if you attend the same conference this year. It is more than a matter of competition for the same resources when you attend the same conference year after year. People tend to stagnate in the face of repetition and we do not have the same energy and enthusiasm when speaking with our colleagues. When you attend a new conference, you meet new prospects for referrals and connections. Who knows, you might also make some new friends!

We excel at the jobs that allow us to focus on our strengths. This concept is addressed in Rule 1.1, entitled, *Competence.* It states, in relevant part, "A lawyer shall provide competent representation to a client." When you increase your competency and at the same time increase your contact list, you and your clients benefit. Follow Robin's advice and you will derive more satisfaction from the tasks you enjoy. Lower your stress and seek more success. That is a world class combination.

2

MAKING IT TO THE GOAL LINE

A goal without an action plan is a daydream.
– Dr. Nathaniel Branden

How often have you set a goal but failed to achieve it?

In Chapter Two, we continue our focus on goal-setting. Chapter One talked about how to set realistic, meaningful goals for your law practice and your life. I gave you some ideas for how to set aside time to plan, how to focus on what is most important, and how to ask yourself ten simple questions that can dramatically change the way you set your goals.

Now we will look at how to build a plan to turn your goals into results. We already know that:

- **People who set goals achieve more than those who don't.**
- **Written goals with an action plan produce the best results.**
- **The rewards for goal setting go far beyond the goals themselves.**
- **Planning how you will achieve your goals is what drives results.**

Now let's go a step further. In their books, *Periodization: 12 Weeks to Breakthrough* and *The 12 Week Year*, Brian Moran and Michael Lennington tell us, "It's not what you know; it's not even who you know; it's what you implement that counts."[1]

In Chapter One, I introduced you to Jinny Ditzler's *BEST YEAR YET* program for setting annual goals. We are accustomed to setting goals on an annual basis, and that process is useful in creating a twelve-month vision for defining results. To actually implement those goals, we have to shift our thinking away from a seemingly endless year where there is plenty of time, to a narrower focus that reinvents what a year *could* look like.

If you are an athlete or know someone who is, then you know that athletes train on short timetables, on what I call a rolling-forward schedule. Athletes typically break their training goals down into twelve-week chunks. There is no year, as we know it; there is only the twelve-week period they are in right now. This system, called Periodization, began as a technique to dramatically improve athletic performance. It emphasizes focus, concentration, and overload on a specific skill or discipline.

Authors Brian Moran and Michael Lennington have taken those training principles and adapted them into a system they call "Strategic Breakthroughs."[2] It is their system for focusing on the critical factors that drive production and life balance. I use this technique for myself and in the work I do with my clients through my Raising the Bar coaching practice. It is the best one I have found for increasing the likelihood that your goals will produce real, tangible results.

---

[1] Brian P. Moran and Michael Lennington, *Periodization: 12 Weeks to Breakthrough* (Holt, MI: Strategic Breakthroughs, 2003), Kindle Edition, chap. "Execution is the Key," para. 2.
[2] Moran and Lennington, *Periodization: 12 Weeks to Breakthrough.*

The Strategic Breakthroughs process is a structured approach that fundamentally changes the way you think and act. By creating urgency around those critical few activities that drive a healthy and successful law practice, you will be executing those core activities daily and weekly at a pace that is sufficient to reach your long-term goals.

I love that idea and have found it to be an exceptionally effective method to consistently achieve results. Three things have to happen, however, for the process to work for you:

1.   **You must *change your mind* about time.**
2.   **You must *orient your plan around principles and disciplines that are aligned* with the achievement of your objectives.**
3.   **You must be *willing* to take the actions you need to take, even when you don't feel like it.**

As you approach the planning process, remember that only you can decide your degree of commitment. That commitment will be measured by the results you obtain.

Because it may be a totally new concept to you, and because it is so important to your success, I'm going to spend a little more time on the process of periodization. Periodization throws out the idea of annualized plans. A year becomes twelve-weeks. The year-end push we all succumb to, therefore, disappears. There is no year-end. There are no quarters. There is only this twelve-weeks.

Under an annualized planning process, you can afford a week or more here and there, where you don't execute or hit your target. But under a twelve-week system, your wiggle room for bad weeks virtually disappears. How many bad weeks can you have in a twelve-week period and still hit your goal? Periodization narrows the focus to *daily and weekly*, which is where execution occurs. The periodization process asks you to really drill down to what is most important in achieving your goals, and to do those things first.

If the periodization process appeals to you, and you would like to use it to change your results right now, visit the Strategic Breakthroughs website at 12weekyear.com. You will find a web-based program that will help you divide your goals into twelve-week and one-week segments. You will even be sent a message each week, reminding you of what you said you wanted to accomplish. Your results will be based on the concept that, if you achieve 85 percent of each week's goals you will achieve your overall goals. This last point is an important one. Accountability is a critical part of your goal planning exercise. Whether it is through a web-based program or working with a partner or coach, a regularly scheduled system of accountability will keep you energized and moving forward.

Your action items for today, that will lead you to success tomorrow, include:

1. **Read *Periodization: 12 Weeks to Breakthrough* and/or *The 12 Week Year*, which are available for purchase at 12weekyear.com.**
2. **Attend a Periodization seminar to learn more.** This is a pricier solution, but if you have a track record of consistently missing your targets it might be a good investment for you.
3. **Use the Strategic Breakthroughs web site to set up your goals and receive weekly reports.**
4. **Keep your plan where you can see it, every day.**

Let's wrap up *Making It To The Goal Line...*

- **Your plan for achieving your goals will drive your results.**
- **You can create a greater sense of urgency by changing your mind about time.** Shifting from an annual to a twelve-week year will dramatically alter how you execute on a daily and weekly basis.
- **Your results will reflect your degree of commitment.**
- **Doing what is most important every day, whether you feel like it or not, will increase your chances of success.**
- **Accountability, whether through an online system, a partner, or a coach, will help you stay focused and consistent in your efforts.**
- **Keeping your plan in plain site will remind you of your goals.**

As Dr. Nathaniel Branden, pioneer in the psychology of self-esteem, says, "A goal without an action plan is a daydream." Daydreams become reality when you plan your work and work your plan.

LEGAL & ETHICAL CONSIDERATIONS

You look around your office in June and wonder where January went! Your desk is piled high with documents, your staff needs your attention and your spouse is insisting that you take some time for your family! As another day evaporates into the ether, you need a way out of the time treadmill that has become your life! That's when it hits you! "If I only had four hours to catch up..." If you are unable to manage your time, it will control your life.

Regarding prioritizing, Rule 1.1 states, as we have mentioned, "A lawyer shall provide competent representation to a client." Comment 6 states, "To maintain the requisite knowledge and skill, a lawyer should engage in continuing study and education." Training in prioritizing, time management and efficiency will improve your skills as a lawyer. After all, competence is about time on task and resolving client problems in an efficient manner. When you learn to prioritize, you reduce the likelihood of missing a deadline and increase your ability to handle client matters properly. This concept is expressed in Comment 2 to Rule 1.5 entitled *Diligence* that reads, "Perhaps no professional shortcoming is more widely resented than procrastination." You and your clients will benefit from your enhanced ability to process work, manage your time and increase your efficiency.

How much time should you spend on client and network development? How will you balance the time demands of bringing in new business and managing business relationships? As you go through this book, you must also keep in mind your obligations to your existing clients.

You have an obligation to stay focused and attend to the matters entrusted to you. Rule 1.3 reads as follows:

A lawyer shall act with reasonable diligence and promptness in representing a client. Reasonable diligence as used in this Rule means that a lawyer shall not without just cause to the detriment of the client in effect willfully abandon or willfully disregard a legal matter entrusted to the lawyer.

So, how will you balance your obligations to your clients and still have time to network, meet with potential clients and work to grow your practice? DELEGATE, DELEGATE, DELEGATE! You simply cannot grow your practice without delegation. You must commit to this process and take the plunge. Read on to find out how.

PART TWO:

INCREASE YOUR PRODUCTIVITY

3

DELEGATION IS KEY TO LEVERAGING YOUR TIME

The greatest loss of time is
delay and expectation . . .
– Seneca

"If it's to be, it's up to me." That might have worked when you were working your way up to your current role, but if you still operate that way, you have positioned yourself for failure. Did that get your attention? If you still want to do everything yourself, it is unlikely that you will ever hit your biggest goals nor will your team ever fulfill its potential without being presented with the chance to do more. Letting go of work that you don't need to do will free you up to focus on what is most important and empower those around you to excel.

In this chapter, I guide you through the process of determining what and how to delegate. You will then be able to keep your eyes firmly fixed on your goals and become a model for your firm that others can follow.

First, let's talk about what delegation is and what it is not. *Webster's* defines the verb *delegate* as "entrusting a task or a responsibility to another person, typically one who is less senior than oneself."[3] The key word here is, of course, "entrusting." It's the *trusting* part that often stops us from moving tasks from our plate to someone else's. That suggests the other problem with delegating—the confusion between delegating and assigning.

When you *assign* a task, it still belongs to you. Someone else is executing the task, but you retain the responsibility for it. Assigning a task is a short-term solution. Nothing has really changed.

When you *delegate*, you move the responsibility for that task to someone else. This frees you up for work that is more important. Your attention can turn to bigger issues. Delegating a task is a long-term solution; and the benefits of delegation do not stop there. When you opt to delegate, you benefit both your firm and yourself. Delegation helps prepare others for more responsibility and it positions them to advance. Offering subordinates the opportunity to take on more responsibility communicates your trust and belief in them and your desire to support their growth. These are important elements in developing strategies for employee retention and succession planning. It is one of the most important things you will do as your firm's leader.

If you are in a solo practice where you are the managing partner and everything else, delegation becomes a more creative process. It requires seeking out appropriate resources on a per-project or ongoing basis.

Earlier, we talked about trust as an obstacle to delegation. There is another objection that you may have about turning work over to someone else—the time it takes to make sure something will be done properly. Yes, it does take time to

---

[3] "Delegate," *Merriam-Webster's Collegiate Dictionary* 11th ed. (Springfield, Mass: Merriam-Webster, 2003) 329.

delegate, to impart information that will ensure the desired result. However, if you are using the time factor to argue against letting go of a project, let me assure you that you need not be concerned. The investment you make on the front end will keep reaping dividends as you move forward.

Yes, it might take time to train someone to take over a task, and it may take some attention and follow-up to guide the transition of responsibility; but in the long run you will have a solution that helps both you and the person to whom you are delegating. That person will be empowered, through increased responsibility, and will get better and better at executing that task. Of course, you must take the time to choose the right task and the right individual to whom you entrust the work.

Choosing what tasks to delegate and to whom requires preparation and analysis. Start by making a list of the tasks you are currently performing. Next, identify those tasks that could, if done by someone else, free you to concentrate on your most important goals. For example, you may be accustomed to driving all the firm's marketing initiatives. Your time would be better-spent meeting with clients or developing strategy. Sort your tasks in order of importance, and look around your organization for likely delegation candidates. Ask yourself five key questions:

- **Is this a task that someone else can do, or is it critical that I do it myself?** Be honest. Could someone else be taught to do it?
- **Can I use this as an opportunity to help others grow and develop their skills?**
- **Is this a task that can be done repeatedly? Can the person assigned to it continue to do it over time.**
- **Do I have enough time to properly prepare the other person to take on this task and be successful doing it?**

23

- **Is this a task I should delegate, or am I just trying to get out of something I really must do myself?** Some tasks, though burdensome, really must remain on your own to-do list.

Two other parts of the delegation equation require your thoughtful attention. They are: accuracy and risk. Must the task be completed perfectly, or is "good enough" sufficient for this task? For instance, is there a consequence for failing to meet a time requirement for this task that would produce a significantly negative result?

As you assess your resources, remember that you don't have to completely let go of control, at least not at first. There are six levels of delegation. You can choose the level that best matches the task. It may depend on your willingness to give the task away and the competence level of the person you select. You can ask that person to:

- **Research and report.**
- **Recommend action.**
- **Take action-when you say GO.**
- **Take action-unless you say NO.**
- **Take action and let you know what was done.**
- **Take action without reporting or involving you again.**

No matter where you start the delegation process, you'll find that people will generally rise to the occasion. As others take on tasks, resist the temptation to fill up all your time with new smaller tasks that simply replace the old ones. Allocate a portion of your newly available time to those activities that are key to reaching your goals.

As important as delegation is to your own success, passing the baton to the right person is just as important to that person's success. A mismatch can result in failure for both of you. There are three critical factors in choosing the right person:

1. **Assess the knowledge and skill level of the person you are considering.**

2. **Be aware of the individual's career objectives, motivations and style.** A person who likes to work independently will resent you if you hover over the task, and someone who needs constant direction and feedback may be too costly, in terms of your time, to be a good choice.

3. **Consider the current workload.** Will this task add so much to the person's workload that nothing will get done, or will it require a complicated restructuring of roles? If you have to move multiple responsibilities around, this may be your opportunity to realign many tasks that will ultimately free you for what is most important.

Finally, here is a ten-step strategy for successful delegation, from MindTools.com:[4]

1. **Clearly articulate the desired outcome.** Begin with the end in mind, and specify the desired results.

2. **Clearly identify constraints, boundaries and lines of authority.**

3. **Include others in the delegation process, empowering them to have input on what tasks are to be delegated to them and when.**

---

[4] "Successful Delegation: Using the Power of Other People's Help," *MindTools*, http://www.mindtools.com/pages/article/newLDR_98.htm

4. **Synchronize responsibility with authority and accountability.**

5. **Delegate down to the lowest possible organizational level.** The people who are closest to the work are best suited for the task. They have the most intimate knowledge of the details of their everyday work.

6. **Provide support.** Be available for questions and for monitoring results.

7. **Focus on results, versus how the work should be done.** Your way, believe it or not, is probably not the only way. Encourage trust and promote success by giving others the room to create their own methods and processes.

8. **Avoid "upward delegation."** If there is a problem, don't allow the person to shift responsibility for the task back to you. Ask for recommended solutions— don't simply provide an answer.

9. **Build motivation and commitment.** Discuss how success will impact the person's financial rewards, future opportunities and other desirable consequences. Provide recognition when deserved.

10. **Build in measurements and controls by discussing timelines and deadlines.** Agree on a schedule of checkpoints and milestones, making appropriate adjustments and reviewing work as it progresses.

Seneca, the Roman stoic philosopher, statesman, and dramatist, reminds us that, "The greatest loss of time is delay and expectation." If you are still struggling with the idea of letting go, time is the price of your delay. Why not expect good results and just do it?

LEGAL & ETHICAL CONSIDERATIONS

The client hired you! That's what you keep telling yourself. They did not want my associates working on their case. You become more concerned about the growing pile of documents that seems to be multiplying exponentially in your inbox! Then you realize, at some point in your career, a senior lawyer began to entrust more projects to you and you rose to the occasion. You needed support and guidance through the process, but you served the client and grew into the lawyer you are today. Delegation is the key to mentoring.

Behind every great lawyer is a great staff. How does a lawyer go from good to great? The greater the lawyer, well, the greater the staff! How does an attorney maximize her time to balance building a practice and attending to client matters? The answer, as Robin points out, is delegation.

However, what can a lawyer delegate without running afoul of the Rules of Professional Conduct? The simple fact and an overarching principle of Robin's chapter is that you cannot do everything, so stop trying to do so!

First and foremost, "a lawyer may not assist in the unauthorized practice of law," according to Rule 5.5. This means that you cannot delegate to a non-lawyer any task that involves the practice of law. Learning to delegate within the parameters of the Rules is an essential skill.

Delegate tasks that do not involve providing legal advice and counseling clients—ALL of them! These include setting appointments, organizing client files, and transmitting documents to and from clients. The nexus between Robin's advice and the Rules lies in making certain that you are *only* personally handling the tasks that *require* your time and attention as an attorney.

27

If you believe that you, and only you, can schedule appointments on your calendar, re-read Chapters 3, 4, and 5 of this book. Buy a crowbar and ask a trusted staff member to help wrestle your calendar out of your hands! The sooner you do so, the sooner you will *find* time to build your practice.

Remember that you are training your staff, including your associates every hour of every day. People learn from focused teaching sessions, from self-directed efforts, and from watching! If you insist on scheduling everything yourself, your staff will learn not to be sensitive to your time because they have no concept of your time! If you never delegate the first draft of a pleading, document, or correspondence, your staff will learn to wait for you to bring them a nearly finished product for a final tweak! The pernicious effect of all this is that your staff will eventually lose the skills for which you hired them! If your skills get rusty, your staff will lose their edge as well.

Worse yet is the lesson you teach your associates when you fail to delegate. They will learn to wait for you to hand them a task instead of learning to take the initiative to tackle the task. Encouraging them to seek out tasks without waiting for you to hand them work to do is the underlying basis and foundation of mentoring them to make rain!

What are the winning delegation rules for senior lawyers mentoring associates? Encourage them to use staff to schedule appointments and manage their schedule. Encourage them to use technology to make it easier for the staff to keep their schedule. Teach them to block out time for tasks, including making time to meet and call potential clients and business leads. Teach them to have the confidence in the staff to involve them early in any process and to learn to work through mistakes and rough patches instead of abandoning their own efforts to delegate.

So, who can perform the tasks that you previously reserved or hoarded? Let's look at the following tricky situation and see how it could be handled: You delegate the scheduling of client appointments to your legal assistant and he calls a client to schedule a deposition. During the call, the client begins to ask for opinions on what documents they should review prior to the deposition.

This is a legal issue, and your staff should be prepared to state that they cannot give advice on those matters. However, you can instruct your staff to take this opportunity to schedule a phone call with the client *when you have time on your calendar* to address the client's question.

Think about the advantages of this technique. First, you have your legal assistant setting appointments while you work on other matters. Second, if *your assistant* calls the client it can be made clear that it is not appropriate to discuss legal issues at this time. If *you* initiate the call to set a deposition date and the client has a question, you will feel a need to address the question immediately. *This five-minute call may end thirty minutes later.* Three calls like that per day and you will be so far behind the time curve that you will never catch up at the end of the day…or by the end of the week. Does this scenario sound familiar?

Another way to prevent this situation is to anticipate any questions that the client may have when they receive a call from your staff. Give the staff member instructions on what to say and what questions they cannot answer for this particular situation. As you and your staff work together, you will streamline this process.

Here is another scenario: Your paralegal is capable and experienced. Are you using that staff member in a way that will maximize your time? It is clear that you cannot allow your paralegal to draft pleadings and client correspondence without your input, or to file pleadings without your approval. However, you can create a bank of legal forms and instruct the paralegal to use those forms to create a first draft of the pleading at issue. This saves time, helps the paralegal gain experience, and stays within legal mandates. It saves immense time in authoring a pleading. Another time saver is to then *schedule a time* to review the draft with the paralegal. Treat this time as you would any other appointment. You will find that your staff will appreciate an uninterrupted slice of your precious time. Better yet, allow the paralegal to place an appointment on your calendar to review the draft!

If you employ these techniques, over time, you will find that deadlines are no longer a frantic race to the mailbox or the courthouse. Remember, time management is not an oxymoron—the more you avoid unplanned meetings and conferences, the more efficient you will become. If you transform the review of draft pleadings and feedback to your staff into scheduled, organized events, you will multiply your efficiency as well as theirs. Spontaneity and time management are diametrically opposed to one another in the practice of law.

Does all this sound foreign to you? If so, start changing now before you are found face down in a pile of deadlines while your staff wonders where you are because you left for an appointment they didn't know about because they do not have access to your calendar!

4

EAT THAT FROG:
Take a Bite Out Of Your To-Do List

Procrastination is the thief of time.
– Edward Young

Brian Tracy tells us in his book, *Eat That Frog: 21 Great Ways to Stop Procrastinating and Get More Done in Less Time*, what Mark Twain once said, that if the first thing you do each morning is to eat a live frog, you can go through the rest of the day with the satisfaction of knowing that you have experienced what is probably the worst thing that is going to happen to you over the next twenty-four hours.[5]

In Chapter Four, I show you how to accomplish your goals by biting into your biggest, hardest, and most difficult tasks first. Disciplining yourself to start there, and persisting until your work is complete, will dramatically improve your effectiveness.

Studies show that for those who get paid more and promoted faster, it is the quality of their action-orientation that

---

[5] Brian Tracy, *Eat That Frog! 21 Great Ways to Stop Procrastinating and Get More Done in Less Time* (San Francisco: Berrett-Koehler Publishers, Inc.), Kindle Edition, "Introduction," 2.

sets them apart. That one specific, observable and consistent behavior positions them for success. The most successful, effective people are those who tackle their major tasks first. They work diligently and single-mindedly until those tasks are complete. This is a life-changing revelation.

No matter what your circumstances, it is not whom you know, nor what you know, that determines your success. It is *how you spend your time.* Of course, choosing the right way to spend your time is not always that easy, is it? If we were to boil the whole concept down to its basic elements, success or failure is simply a result of the habits we create. In this case, we're talking about the habits of focus and concentration. There are three "Ds" to building those habits: decision, discipline, and determination:

1. **You must make the *decision* to develop a habit of completing your most difficult tasks first.** However, a decision is meaningless until you act.
2. **You must have the *discipline* to build new habits, by practicing again and again until you master them.**
3. **You must act with conscious *determination*, until the habit is locked in and becomes a permanent part of your thought process.**

The amount of time required to complete an important job is often the same as the time required to do an *un*important one. Before beginning any work, ask yourself, "Is this task in the top 20 percent of my activities; or is it in the bottom 80 percent?" Making the right choice will give you a tremendous feeling of pride and satisfaction. You will be accomplishing something of value and significance. Completing a low-value task gives you none of that, even if it consumes the same amount of time and energy. When in doubt about which task or project to put at the top of your list, imagine you are about to leave town for a month. *What would you absolutely make sure* *you got done before you left?* Whatever your answer, get busy right now and get it done!

To determine a pecking order of your to-dos, ask yourself:

- **What are my highest value activities?**
- **What can I do that, if done well, will make a real difference?**
- **What is the most valuable use of my time right now? What is my biggest frog of all?**

Applying yourself to getting things done in the right order means training yourself like an athlete. If you want to consistently perform at the top of your game, regardless of what it is, you must set your standard higher than anyone else. You must prepare your mind and body for the rigors of the activity, even if you are in an office environment. Feed yourself as you would feed a world class athlete before a competition. Build your physical stamina through exercise and get proper rest. Take your health and fitness pulse by asking yourself:

- **What am I doing physically that I should do more?**
- **What am I doing that I should do less?**
- **What am I not doing that I should start doing if I want to perform at my best?**
- **What am I doing today that I should stop doing altogether?**

Practice saying "NO" to anything that is not a valuable use of your time and your life. If you find that the word "NO" has disappeared from your lexicon, practice saying it aloud right now. Pledge to say "NO" to anything that may simply fill up your spare time, because spare time for you is a myth. You simply do not have any extra time to do what does not need to be done. Your dance card is full.

When it comes to rest, and by *rest* I really mean sleep, we all seem to think less sleep and more work is the badge of accomplishment. It is as if we can claim a great distinction among our peers by how hard we drive ourselves on as little fuel as possible. Fully rested, you can get two, three or even five times more accomplished than when you are tired. One extra hour of sleep every night can literally change your life.

If the thought of adding an extra hour of sleep is disturbing to you (I can hear you arguing with me, even as I tell you this), then consider what *taking one full day off* every week could do. Yipes! Are you shaking in your boots? Imagine twenty-four hours every week—even excluding reading, emails, catching up on things at work, or doing anything else that strains your mind. Taking this time will re-charge and re-energize you. That extra boost of energy will help you overcome procrastination and stay on target.

"Procrastination is the thief of time," said early English poet Edward Young. Even in the seventeenth century, people were aware of the high cost of putting things off. However, procrastination can sometimes be a good thing. Let's look at it from a fresh perspective.

Unconscious procrastination is putting off that which is most important or has the most significant long-term consequences. *Creative* procrastination is a thoughtful process that postpones, perhaps forever, what you have decided you are not going to do right now.

To differentiate unconscious from creative procrastination, ask yourself, "Is this something I would not start today, knowing what I now know?" Your answer will automatically route that project or task into the "Do It Now" or the "Creative Procrastination" basket.

Let's review seven practical steps for eating that frog every workday:

1. **At the end of your workday, or on the weekend, make a list of everything you have to do the next day.**
2. **Apply the 20/80 Rule, ranking your list in order of importance.**
3. **Select the job or task that has the most serious potential consequences if you do or don't get it done.**
4. **Gather everything you will need to start and finish this task and lay it out, ready for you to start working on it in the morning.**
5. **Clear your workspace completely so that you have this one, most important task, sitting on your desk in the morning, ready for you to bite into it.**
6. **Train yourself to get up, get ready, walk in, sit down, and start on that task.** Do it without interruption, before you do anything else.
7. **Build your new behavior into a habit, by doing it every day for twenty-one consecutive days.** You will double your productivity in less than a month when you do.

Engage wholeheartedly in this time-management make-over by reminding yourself that what you are doing is just for today—that *just for today* you will plan, prepare and start on your most difficult task before you do anything else.

If you have to eat a live frog, it doesn't pay to sit and look at it for very long. Just go ahead and put worst things first. As

Goethe said, "The things that matter most must never be at the mercy of the things that matter least."

For more on managing procrastination, take a look at *Eat That Frog: 21 Great Ways to Stop Procrastinating and Get More Done in Less Time* by Brian Tracy, or drop by his website at www.briantracy.com.

LEGAL & ETHICAL CONSIDERATIONS

The client and the project seemed interesting. You also believed you handled similar cases in the past and this would give you an opportunity to delve into this practice area again. Then, without much warning, the project became the issue you always seemed to find a way to avoid. You never abandoned the client, but his project always seemed to slip down a few notches on the priority list. This is the proverbial slippery slope and it may not end well for the client or the lawyer.

Every lawyer encounters a client with whom the representation does not work out well. Although this is a part of business, it is perhaps one of the most difficult situations you will encounter. More important to the present topic, there are few situations that will sap the resources and enthusiasm out of your practice more than a client matter that does not belong in your practice!

As a lawyer, you may decide that a particular client is undesirable from the standpoint of the amount of time required to work with him, you find that the client is a disproportionate drain on your services, or quite frankly, you do not enjoy the work. How do you properly pass the representation to another lawyer? Fortunately, the Rules address this situation.

Rule 1.16 provides several scenarios wherein an attorney would seek to terminate the attorney-client relationship. Of course, the attorney can cancel the relationship if the client perpetrates a fraud or lies to his counsel. You should also know, that "a lawyer may withdraw from representing a client if withdrawal can be accomplished without material adverse effect on the interests of the client." The Rule further states that the attorney is not required to provide a reason for withdrawing or ending the representation. This is premised upon the independence of the attorney and the need to allow withdrawal while protecting client confidentiality. In addition, an attorney may discharge a client who refuses to follow legal advice.

If you discharge a client, you should ensure that the client is properly provided with the tools and information necessary to continue his case. Further, if a case is pending in court, you *must* obtain permission of the court before withdrawing. There is one caveat, pursuant to Rule 1.16(c), "The Court can prevent the attorney from withdrawing." As a practice point, your local court rules and the relevant state or federal rules will also likely set out a strict procedure for you to follow when seeking to withdraw from a pending case. Review them carefully *before* you begin the process.

Discharging a client is a difficult decision and can be an arduous process. Regardless of the reasons that drive the decision, after the discharge you should take the opportunity to reflect upon the *start* of the relationship. Was there a disconnect between you and the client? Was the disconnect a personality issue? Was this a case or a client that you never should have accepted? The best way to avoid the work that drains your energy is to screen those clients and cases thoroughly *before* you take the first steps down the path of representation. Are you having a hard time finding the time to discover and meet with prospective clients? Get rid of those problem clients and you will find the time you need!

This brings up important issues for the lawyers you are training and mentoring. The worst impression to give a new associate is any client is a good client! Nothing could be further from the truth! Spend the time reviewing the elements of a good and durable attorney-client relationship. This will not only help your associates screen clients, they will learn how to target potential clients to maximize their rainmaking efforts!

5

MANAGE YOUR MEETING TIME
(Your Partners Will Thank You For It!)

*A meeting is an event at which
the minutes are kept and the hours are lost.*
– Gourd's Axiom

If you believe that "a meeting is an event at which the minutes are kept and the hours are lost," then you won't be surprised to learn that, of the 11 million meetings that take place every day in the US, over 50 percent of the time spent meeting is wasted. Research shows that most professionals attend 61.8 meetings per month. Isn't that astounding? Assuming each of these meetings is one hour long, those individuals lose an average of thirty-one hours per month in unproductive or non-billable time. That's the equivalent of four workdays. Stunning! When you consider that time is our most valuable resource, isn't it about time that we stopped wasting it on meetings?

In this chapter, I'm stepping onto my soapbox about meetings. I will be showing you how to use meetings to meet your goals, make them more useful and productive and ensure that they are worth the investment of your time and talent, as well as the time and talent for the rest of your firm.

Let's start by asking what really goes on at a meeting. Survey results say that 91 percent of professionals who meet on a regular basis spend part of that meeting time daydreaming, 96 percent miss meetings altogether, with 95 percent missing parts of meetings. Bringing other work to a meeting is the guilty admission of 73 percent, 39 percent admit to dozing off during a meeting—and those are just the ones who will own up to it![6]

So why do we even have meetings? With technology serving our communication needs, must we meet? The answer is yes. There are some very good reasons to meet, which technology only reinforces. Here's what I mean:

Telephone tag is one very compelling reason to meet: you call and leave a message, they call and leave a message, you call back and leave a reply, they call back and respond. And so it goes, wasting time and accomplishing—what? Maybe it's time for a meeting!

The same thing happens with email. Around and around you go—with the threads getting further and further down the page—and the effort required to compose an endless string of responses taking longer and longer. Maybe it's time for a meeting!

It's time to re-think the whole meeting concept, to turn your team's "Ugh, it's a meeting" into "Wow, it's a meeting!" Face-to-face meetings can actually speed things up; but how do you know when it's time to meet? There are four criteria for determining if a meeting will work best:

---

[6] Verizon Conferencing White Paper, "Meetings in America, A study of trends, costs and attitudes toward business travel, teleconferencing, and their impact on productivity," (Greenwhich, CT: INFOCOMM, 1998), https://e-meetings.verizonbusiness.com/global/en/meetingsinamerica/uswhitepaper.php

1. **You have a specific goal or objective that only a meeting will facilitate.**
2. **You have an agenda that will focus your discussion and it will also help those with whom you are meeting to prepare for something in the future.**
3. **Key individuals who are crucial to the outcome will be able to attend.**
4. **The topics to be discussed cannot be handled through any other means.**

The *Harvard Business School Communication Newsletter* suggests that the only real reason to have a meeting is to do something together that you can't do better alone. There are only three purposes for having a meeting: to take action by communicating, administering, and deciding.[7]

Whatever the meeting driver, your meeting will be more successful and productive when you factor in the following essential elements:

- **The first is the *time* factor**—time as it relates to scheduling and time as it may actually play out. Most meetings tend to be scheduled in multiples of thirty minutes, even if the subject doesn't require that much time. Make your meetings more effective by approaching time as a block of any size you want to make it, as long as it is enough time to accomplish your objectives: five minutes, ten minutes, forty minutes or longer. In some companies, meetings can be quite spontaneous, with the individuals involved text messaging each other to designate a meeting place and time where they come together briefly, accomplish

---

[7] Harvard Business Communication: A Newsletter From Harvard Business School "10 Commandments of Meeting," November 1, 1999.

their objective, and return to other tasks. If it will only take five minutes to achieve your goal, then set the meeting for that time frame and stick with it. (HINT: Know when to stop talking!) You can also call a meeting where no time limit is set. It's often better to plan a meeting that may require participants to stay until the goal is achieved, versus setting an arbitrary time that will surely be exceeded. Make sure that you manage expectations about time, so participants are prepared for the long haul when they are invited to attend.

- **The second is the *leadership* factor.** Meetings are an opportunity to demonstrate leadership, but that can be a double-edged sword. It's important to keep the meeting on track. If you don't, your reputation as a leader can suffer. Take for example, the "long-winded, contentious self-serving" leader or person who takes over the meeting. Many firms use a neutral third-party facilitator to keep things moving when a meeting may be tough to manage. That's a great idea. It takes you off the hot seat in tense situations.

- **Then there's the *preparation* factor.** Planning and distributing an agenda prior to the meeting helps others prepare and stay on track.

The *Harvard Business School Communication Newsletter*[8] offers some additional sage advice on the subject of meetings:

- **Always know what time it is.** Start on time and end on time. Resist the temptation to fill up all the time allotted if you've achieved your goal in less time. End the meeting early if there is nothing more to discuss.

---

[8] Harvard Business Communication: A Newsletter From Harvard Business School "10 Commandments of Meeting," November 1, 1999.

- **Remember the main reason for your meeting.** Stay focused and avoid becoming distracted with extraneous topics, questions or debates. Schedule separate meetings to cover those topics if they are sufficiently important to require further discussion.

- **Refrain from publicly criticizing anyone in the meeting or allowing anyone else to do so.** Steer the conversation back to the main purpose of the meeting. Save any negative comments for a private conversation later.

- **Unless it's an emergency, schedule meetings during normal business hours only.** Promote good will, encourage participation, and demonstrate that you, too, have a life outside of work, by scheduling meetings on company time.

- **Don't use meetings to pressure others into agreement.** Group pressure is a powerful tactic and can be used very effectively to coerce agreement, especially in situations where jobs are at stake. Yes, it might work; but the downside is a work environment where ethics are iffy and the morale compass points downward.

- **Don't use meetings to destroy another person's career.** This goes for you as the leader or as the participant. The transient nature of today's workforce can make it "seem" like this kind of behavior has no consequences for the person doing the destruction, but your reputation as someone who behaves that way will certainly precede you wherever your career takes you.

- **Keep business and personal socializing distinct.** While it is good to have friendly conversations, banter, or chitchat at the start and end of the meeting, it becomes counter-productive when it reveals favorites or inside information that only you and some of the others share.

- **Don't use the power of your position to force a decision you want.** If the decision has already been made, send a memo. If it is up for discussion, have a meeting and use your role as leader to bring the group to consensus.

- **Always distribute a clear agenda before the meeting.** It is the roadmap that will take your meeting where you want it to go, and it gives others the opportunity to prepare.

- **Discontinue standing meetings when their reason for being no longer exists.** Revisit standing meetings on a regular basis. If you no longer need to meet, then don't.

In addition, here are a few more ideas from my own archives:

- **Invite only those who need to be there.** The more people in attendance, the more likely it is that the discussion will break down and decisions will be delayed. Meetings function best with six participants at most.

- **Diffuse digressions with an idea bin.** Use a flipchart or whiteboard to list all ideas the meeting generates. Use a separate flipchart for ideas that are not directly related to the meeting's goals. These can be used to acknowledge other subjects without letting them derail the primary conversation. Schedule subsequent discussions on these topics, if appropriate.

- **Summarize all meeting action plans**. Recap all agreements, assignments and decisions at the end of the meeting, and follow up with a written summary that pins down agreed-upon action, assignments and deadlines.

"All these tips are useful," you might say. "But how can I empower the other members of my firm to make a meeting more productive?" Show others how to facilitate efficiency by suggesting that they help prepare the agenda, take notes, act as timekeeper, or prepare the final summary. You will help them increase their visibility in a positive way and make the experience more productive for everyone in the room. Show your team that, if they can't get out of the meeting, then at least they can get more out of it.

LEGAL & ETHICAL CONSIDERATIONS

You hired good staff. You hired lawyers who attended good schools. You took great care to make the firm run smoothly. So, why are your staff members in your office asking for direction? Why are your young attorneys cutting their deadlines close? Where is the direction and momentum you felt last quarter? The short answer is that people need direction on a regular basis. No matter how talented and dedicated your team, you need to spend time putting the train back on the tracks.

We owe it to our clients to use our time efficiently. Therefore, if you are billing for "wasted time" you are not serving your client's interests. You may also run afoul of the mandate that your fee must always be reasonable. Rule 1.5 requires lawyers to "act with reasonable diligence and promptness in representing a client." Rule 1.3 says that you cannot meet these guidelines in endless meetings that have no direction. You owe it to your clients to take charge of the meeting process. Ensure that each meeting follows an agenda. Meetings devoid of purpose and direction waste valuable time that you could devote to your clients. Stop scheduling those useless meetings and you'll be able to start scheduling time for the other parts of your life.

To be fair, most law firms have the opposite problems when it comes to meeting with staff. I highly recommend a weekly meeting with all attorneys and staff on your team. I do this every week. We confine the meetings to forty-five minutes and begin with a recitation of the deadlines in play for that week and the next. This allows for reallocation of resources as necessary. We also discuss any new cases so any staff member can field a client inquiry enough to take the call, receive the information, and set up a follow up call with an attorney, if necessary. In short, no one in your office or group should be in the dark about any matter and no client should be required to make two calls to get an answer or schedule a time to speak with the attorney handling her case.

I also meet with the attorneys in my office for one hour each week and each staff member for thirty minutes each week. Those individual meetings are reserved for status updates on projects, feedback on performance, and forecasting projects for the next few weeks. I spend time with each employee to ensure they understand the type of cases we handle and what a good potential client "looks like." After all, legal assistants and paralegals go to parties, spend time with family members, and meet people in need of legal services.

When meeting with the attorneys, it is important to tell them how much time you personally spent on client development that week. This is more than leading by example. These conversations will generate questions and get them thinking about potential clients. I love to hear these words from an associate, "I have a friend who just opened a business and they need a lawyer for [something outside our practice area.]" At that point, I tell the associate how to contact their friend and make a referral to an attorney who has helped our firm in the past. I encourage the associate to call the attorney and advise they are referring a client to them. This puts the associate in a mindset of looking for these connections that lead to future business. In the space of fifteen minutes, a colleague has a new client, my associate has become a resource for a new business owner, and my associate has seen first-hand how the referral engine works.

Meetings with staff can become a "time vacuum." Make certain you are prepared to end the meeting and keep order. Sometimes a side conversation with a staff member is needed to keep the future meetings on track. However, meetings are here to stay and are a necessary part of our profession. If you find that your day is getting off track with client meetings, consider this: if you are unable to control the agenda, flow and duration of a staff meeting, are you surprised that your meetings with clients ramble on?

6

PLAN EXTENDED TIME OFF:
Build a Sabbatical Into Your Law Practice to Re-energize Your Rainmaking

Just say "NO."

Have you found yourself daydreaming about what it would be like to chuck your workaday world and head out on a great adventure? Perhaps you would like to stop working long enough to lend your time and talent to a favorite charitable cause. How about just doing nothing? Does the idea of that fire you up?

In this chapter, we explore how you can make the time to refresh and enrich your life (and make you a better rainmaker) through a sabbatical.

Dubbed "the world's best perk," sabbaticals are rapidly becoming a part of the world of business. Once a benefit reserved exclusively for the academic world, sabbaticals now offer businesses an additional lure for recruiting and retention.

A sabbatical is a prolonged interval, typically one year ("Robin, you must be kidding!") in the career of an individual that is taken in order to fulfill some specific goal, like writing a book or traveling extensively for research. Sabbaticals are generally paid breaks offered by academic institutions. In the business world, sabbaticals are becoming popular for providing a career break and are usually, but not always, unpaid.

Today, 4 percent of large companies offer paid sabbaticals to their employees, and 15 percent offer unpaid sabbaticals, according to the Society for Human Resource Management.[9] Consider that if you work a forty-hour week for forty-nine weeks a year over a forty-year career, you have invested 78,400 hours in your work, not including the extra hours you know you put in. Is a sabbatical starting to look pretty good right now?

Thankfully, today's sabbaticals are not reserved exclusively for the employee with long service. In the United Kingdom, where 20 percent of companies have a career break policy and 10 percent are considering it, young professionals are being granted sabbaticals as a break from work in order to determine if their career path is correct for them. Imagine where you might be today if you had that option when you were first starting out! (Would you have chosen the law? Would you be the managing partner?)

In a survey conducted by a creative staffing firm with the Tuck School of Business at Dartmouth University, American professionals indicated a strong interest in sabbaticals, with 68 percent of women and 58 percent of men saying they would consider taking an extended leave from work.[10]

---

[9] A Research Report by the Society of Human Resource Management (SHRM), "2011 Employee Benefits: Examining Employee Benefits Amidst Uncertainty."
[10] John Rossheim, "Take a Sabbatical Without Derailing Your Career," Monster.com, referencing an online study conducted by Aquent and the Tuck School of Business Management at Dartmouth.

If you had the chance to take a sabbatical, would you? If your answer is yes, let's hear the arguments.

"Robin, I would love to take a sabbatical, but how in the world can I break away from my work long enough to benefit from what a sabbatical might do for me?"

Good question, and one I would expect you to ask. I have a one-word, two-letter strategy that will throw the door open for you and perhaps yield more than you imagined it could. It is a strategy that I use myself but one that I had to discipline myself to use. It is how I was able to take the whole month of July off in order to pursue other important interests. As anti-drug initiatives used to urge, "Just say 'NO'." I'll bet you are shuddering right now at the prospect of it. Saying NO is one of the hardest lessons many of us will have to learn. Being prepared to say NO, when it is the right thing to do for yourself, will give you the space to imagine what a sabbatical year could do for you. Perhaps you think the law is a profession where sabbaticals are impossible. You may be surprised to learn what some firms are doing in that regard as reported by Jeanne Sahadi, senior writer for CNNMoney.com.[11]

- American Express employees with at least ten years of service can apply for a paid sabbatical, lasting one to six months, to work for a non-profit or school of their choice.
- After seven years with the investment firm American Century, employees can take a four-week paid sabbatical, in addition to any vacation time they may have accrued.
- Since 1986, partners in the law firm Alston & Bird are entitled to a paid sabbatical for up to four months,

---

[11] Jeanne Sahadi, "The World's Best Perk", CNNMoney, June 13, 2006, http://money.cnn.com/2006/06/13/commentary/everyday/sahadi/index.htm

depending on their age and tenure. (If they can do it, then why not you and your firm?)

- Goldman Sachs launched a public service sabbatical program in 2004. Their managing directors, vice presidents, and executive directors are allowed a year of paid leave to work with a charitable, public service, or cultural organization of their choosing.

If you are intrigued and at least open to the possibility, then John Rossheim, senior contributing writer for monster.com offers these tips on how to plan for and take a sabbatical:[12]

- **Learn about your firm's sabbatical policy, if it has one. Or, why not introduce one?** The first place to look is the employee manual, but that is not the ultimate guide. (HINT: Delegate someone to research this for you!) It's possible your firm has a policy but it hasn't caught up with the manual yet.

- **Prepare a positive pitch.** It's important that you keep your interest in a sabbatical to yourself while you formulate your pitch. Carefully write down what you want to do, why you want to do it, and when you will return, *before* exploring the idea further. Be sure to use the word "sabbatical." It's a word with power and strength attached to it. "Sabbatical" says you have a plan; and it also raises the bar on the firm's expectations. How will it benefit you *and* them? Be sure you can live up to what you propose. By the way, working with a coach can help you shape your plan and give you an edge in pleading your case.

- **Think creatively.** If your firm does not have a formal sabbatical or extended leave program, and you still want to ask for one, you may have to look for an

---

[12] John Rossheim, "Take a Sabbatical Without Derailing Your Career."

opportunity to negotiate. Perhaps you can time your request to coincide with a raise or bonus, asking if you can have, say, two months time off, instead of the money. You might also suggest that what you will be doing could be a great public relations opportunity for building good press about the practice. In addition, the state of the economy could make an unpaid leave attractive to the firm, giving it a chance to save some money now, with the opportunity for you to return at a pre-agreed upon date when conditions will hopefully have improved.

- **Keep in touch while you are away.** Wherever your sabbatical takes you in the world, checking in from time to time will keep you in your firm's thoughts. You might even consider doing a project, just to keep your hand in the work-world. Technology makes communication easier from even the most remote parts of the planet. Dashing off a note on how things are going, with pictures, will keep people involved. A blog or online journal that your colleagues can follow will make others feel a part of what you are doing. They'll even be able to cheer you on.

- **Keep your skills sharp and ready for your return.** That same study I mentioned earlier reveals that 61 percent of hiring managers welcome workers who have been on extended leave in order to update their skills. Keep that in mind as you choose how you will spend your sabbatical time; and don't forget to keep your professional memberships and licenses current.

One final thought about sabbaticals: make a commitment to take one right now, and start planning for it. When I made that commitment to myself, it took months of planning, preparation and saying NO to free up an entire month for what I wanted to do. The next year it was easier, because I knew what those four weeks did for me, and I couldn't wait to have them again. A sabbatical for me has now become an annual event. Clients and colleagues know that I will be off-line for those four weeks and are eager to hear what I've been up to when I return (and more than a little jealous).

LEGAL & ETHICAL CONSIDERATIONS

"I'll relax later." "I'll get a vacation after the first of the year." "My family understands; I've got a lot on my plate." Ever hear these excuses? Ever used them?

If you search the internet for "lawyers stress statistics," you will find more than 100,000 articles, websites, and links. There are books, seminars, and testimonials, as well as resources outlined on the websites of several state bar associations. One common theme ties the statistics, recommendations, and cautionary tales together: the practice of law is a demanding and stressful profession.

If you have not done so already, you will soon learn that the time you spend "off task" is just as important as the time you spend "on task." There are no surprises here for anyone who has been practicing law for a while. However, consider these statistics from lawyer and author Gerald LeVan in *Lawyers' Lives Out of Control: A Quality of Life Handbook*[13]:

- 40 percent of lawyers and graduates of law schools do not practice law.
- At least 25 percent of all lawyers regret their choice of a profession and would drop out if they could find suitable employment.
- More than 25 percent would discourage their children from becoming a lawyer.

Even more alarming is stress that can lead to depression or suicide. Michael J. Sweeney wrote *The Devastation of Depression: Lawyers are at Greater Risk.* It's an impairment to take seriously. In this article, published on the American Bar

---

[13] Gerald LeVan, *Lawyers Lives Out of Control: A Quality of Life Handbook* (LeVan Co, 1993).

Association web site, Sweeney states that some of the top law-related stressors that can lead to depression are time constraints, deadlines and the depletion of energy that comes from high demands, strong focus and the need to stay on task.

With all the resources available and warning signs as big as billboards, why do lawyers suffer and allow stress to ruin their lives? The simple answer may be too complicated for these pages. However, there are resources to help. The Georgia Bar provides a Lawyer Assistance Program, available to members of the bar twenty-four hours per day. The program includes pre-paid counseling and assistance. All requests for assistance are confidential. You can reach the program via the Georgia Bar website or by calling 800-327-9631.

How many attorneys spend time with their new lawyers to explain the dangers of burnout or excessive stress? In my experience, this is rarely done because the new lawyer and the seasoned lawyer combine at the start of the employment relationship to form a synergistic resistance to the reality of the stress of practicing law. Consider the perspectives of the players in this scenario.

The Associate

We have the new associate or the lawyer who is new to your firm. She is anxious to get going and prove you made the right hiring decision and exceed expectations. This is especially true of new law graduates who have had enough of the theoretical and bar preparation. They want to sink their teeth into a "real" legal matter, irrespective of the practice area. They are willing to work long hours, evenings, weekends, and through mudslides, solar flares, and earthquakes to get the job done. Their chief complaint is "I only billed twenty-two hours yesterday! Give me another project!"

The Seasoned Lawyer

Six months prior to hiring the new associate, you thought you were going to die! You had more deadlines than a news editor, more paper on your desk than Bob Cratchit, and more appointments on your calendar than a barber at boot camp! You were up all night trying to catch up, running around all day trying to keep up, and drinking gallons of coffee trying to stay up! On top of all this, you had to find time to find a lawyer to help! The LAST topic on your mind is telling this heaven-sent worker bee to take a long weekend, spend more time at home, or schedule a vacation sometime this year!

What makes this worse, is that most seasoned lawyers will find more work to fill the time freed up by the efforts of the new associate! One year down the road, the associate looks like you did before you hired her, she has learned that vacations are things that only doctors take, and the reason lawyers have family pictures on their desks is to make certain they see them at some point! This cycle is truly vicious!

Your body, your mind, and your soul need rest. I do not mean an occasional good night of restful sleep. I mean a week off. I have become the master of the three and four day weekends. However, I know that to truly disconnect and charge my batteries, I must get away for one solid week...or more. Whenever I forget this fact and try to cut short that full week or allow work to interrupt that week, I pay the price. Your family also deserves to have quality time with you away from the office and without competing with your laptop for attention!

Consider the hazard of failing to take time off and failing to instill this principle in your new lawyers. We are all more difficult to work with when we are tense, tired, and out of steam. We have all heard of associates who leave a firm because they were always inundated with work and never got a break. When your new associate leaves for this reason, you have done a disservice to your staff who must now shoulder the new burdens: yourself because you must now repeat the process of finding someone new, and your associate who will go to another firm and learn that the volume of the work was not the problem. It was the lack of downtime that led to discord.

Finally, Rule 6.1 states, "A lawyer should aspire to render at least (50) hours of pro bono publico legal services per year." You can recharge your batteries a little bit at a time or through one week helping others. I have received far more in rejuvenation from volunteer work than I ever imagined. You should share this philosophy with your associates. Our profession supports and thrives upon the innate desire of lawyers to help others. You should encourage the younger lawyers in your firm to find their own cause they can serve throughout their careers.

Stress, divorce, substance abuse, depression and burnout cause an alarming number of lawyers to leave our profession every year. Learn to recognize the signs in your colleagues and in yourself and teach the new lawyers how to avoid these issues. Take the problems seriously; take Robin's advice, and *take a sabbatical!*

7

RECOGNIZE AND APPRECIATE YOUR STAFF

*Contrary to what you might believe,
your administrative professionals are not panting
for flowers, candy and a nice lunch. What they
really want is to be a recognized
part of the firm's success.*

Every year, all around the world, during the last full week of April, businesses stop to recognize administrative professionals and the contributions they make to the success towards which we are all working. Wednesday of that week is set aside for special events and recognition as Administrative Professionals Day. It's not too early to be thinking about how you will recognize your administrative professionals when you need to. In this chapter, we look at how to make this potentially high impact event become a more meaningful experience for you and your administrative professionals by committing to making them a more strategic partner in your success and the success of the firm.

Let's start with a little history. The term *secretary* has now come to be called administrative professional. It was derived from the Latin word *secemere*, meaning "to distinguish" or "to set apart." It eventually came to mean someone who was responsible for overseeing business in a confidential manner, usually for a powerful individual. Men dominated the field from the Renaissance until the invention of the typewriter in the 1880s. That's when more women entered the work world as secretaries. Since World War I, the role of the secretary has been more associated with women than men, but the work of the secretary and its newest sobriquet, administrative professional, is by no means populated by women only.

Administrative Professionals Week has been observed every year since 1952. Originally organized as National Secretaries Week, it was the brainchild of the National Secretaries Association, in conjunction with Harry Klemfuss, of Young and Rubicam, and a consortium of office products companies. It was Klemfuss, back in the day, who designed the week to promote the values and importance of the job of secretary. Through his vision, he has raised the stature of secretaries around the world and created an image of the administrative professional as an attractive career. The International Association of Administrative Professionals (IAAP) is now a 40,000 plus member organization with nearly 600 chapters worldwide. [14]

Let's face it, where would any of us be without the organization, dedication, and know-how of the administrative staff that has supported each and every one of us at one time or another over the years?

Now let's turn our attention to the rewards and recognition at the heart of this event. Perhaps, about now, you are thinking, "Thanks, Robin, for reminding me. I'll just run out and get a card, maybe a pre-fab bunch of flowers would be nice, oh, and

---

[14] International Association of Administrative Professionals (IAAP), "When did Administrative Professionals Week begin?" http://www.iaap-hq.org/events/apw/faq

yeah, a lunch (with me!) might be good, too." *Too bad you can't delegate the task to your admin...if you could, they just might give you an earful on what they think about that!*

Contrary to what you might believe, your administrative professionals are not panting for flowers, candy, and a nice lunch. Nor are they desperate for massages, gift cards for dinner or—Oh, NO you didn't—self-help books or time management systems! On the other hand, a carefully chosen assortment of chocolates for a chocolate lover, a gift card to a local nursery for an avid gardener, or a gift card for dinner at a favorite restaurant for a foodie will make a lasting impression. A booklover might really appreciate a gift card to Barnes & Noble or Amazon.com. A dog or cat fancier might relish a gift card from PetSmart. What's important is to take the time to make it personal and meaningful. When in doubt, it's a good idea to ask your firm's administrator or the individual's own significant other for suggestions.

You might be interested to know what administrative professionals have said they really want, even though their wants and needs very seldom translate into what firms and individuals do to recognize them.

When surveyed, most administrative support staff said they prefer observances that recognize their professional role or provide opportunities for professional growth. The IAAP suggests that employers consider these ideas[15]:

- Hold a firm-wide observance or special event for administrative staff, such as a presentation by a professional development speaker, or a group recognition of administrative professionals by the managing partner.

---

[15] International Association of Administrative Professionals (IAAP), "What is the best way to celebrate Administrative Professionals Week?" http://www.iaap-hq.org/events/apw/faq

- Provide registration for a professional development seminar to build the individual's technical, interpersonal, or business skills.
- Support membership in appropriate networking and professional associations.
- Encourage study for and attainment of professional certification.

Additional gift suggestions include appropriate business-related items...hey, an iPhone or Blackberry might be nice...or a monetary bonus for exemplary performance. Just be sure that it's something that is really wanted. By the way, candy, flowers and lunches? They were dead last on the list.

You might be muttering to yourself now, that the firm plans to take care of all this, and "Why should I bother?" Please. Please. Please. Don't pass the buck! It brands you as selfish, and lacking in appreciation and respect for the important work your administrative staff provides. Am I being too hard on you? Maybe you don't fall into the category of uncaring oaf. But, believe me, I have heard too many horror stories from shocked, disappointed, and under-appreciated support staff to think these things don't happen. They do, and these incidents are contributing factors to attrition, overall low productivity, and depleted morale. No one wants to feel his or her work is of so little value that a carelessly selected card, generally chosen by someone else and tossed on the desk, is enough to keep them motivated throughout the year. Bah! The truth is, your firm's gift of recognition may not always hit the mark. Your administrative staff wants to know that the person for whom they work diligently all year (that would be you) cares about them.

Here's an idea that costs nothing but can mean everything: a hand-written note. Add to your gift-giving strategy a hand-written note that is heart-felt and expresses your sincere appreciation and gratitude. It makes a brilliant finishing touch.

Just because there is one "official" day set aside to recognize your administrative staff, you don't have to limit yourself. There are many opportunities throughout the year to recognize your admins. Build reminders into your calendar for service anniversaries, birthdays, and other important milestones, just as you would your planned business development activities or other important commitments. Remembering these events will help create a working environment that inspires loyalty and commitment.

Now that I've laid the groundwork for you to seize the moment when it presents itself to recognize your administrative professionals, let me plant the most important seed. You have an amazing resource sitting (usually) right outside your door. How can you better leverage that resource to benefit you both?

LEGAL & ETHICAL CONSIDERATIONS

They help us when we need to be in two places at once. They work through conflicts that we could never resolve and help us turn a day of chaos into productive and profitable hours! Your staff is the foundation of your practice. Neglect the foundation, the building will crumble.

There are no Rules stressing the importance of the principles and guidance Robin offers in this chapter. It just makes common sense. Your staff facilitates the services you provide to your clients. Keep them informed, keep them empowered, and keep them happy! Treat your staff as fellow professionals and the rest will be easy.

Now the hard part: have you taken the time to teach your associates the importance of working with staff, recognizing staff contributions to the team, and most important, how to get along with staff? I hear so often that lawyers "need to make some staff changes" or "the people in my office just can't get along." If you are going to impart upon your associates the skills they will need to pursue a successful career practicing law, you *must* teach them to manage, motivate, and work with staff.

Attorneys come from varied backgrounds. Some go straight through college and law school and others have a career or two prior to going to law school. They may have little or no experience—or worse, horrific experiences—working with staff. You cannot assume that the new attorneys in your office know how to give staff a project with an appropriate deadline or how to follow up on a task without appearing condescending. These are skills, like rainmaking, that must be taught.

One last word of advice from inside the trenches; staff are *never* expendable. The disruption of replacing staff members is incalculable and turnover will earn your firm a reputation of a place that no one wants to work. One attorney had the reputation of having an ejection seat behind the legal assistant's desk. If you find yourself going through staff more often than your peers, perhaps the problem lies behind your desk.

Work hard to build and maintain staff relationships and even harder to repair them when necessary. Your staff members are the first and last impression your clients and potential clients receive. They are the lifeblood of your practice.

PART THREE:

MAXIMIZE YOUR NEW AND OLD RELATIONSHIPS

8

REINVENT YOUR NETWORKING STRATEGIES FOR LONG TERM RESULTS

Good things happen to people who make good things happen.
– Bob Littell

Is relationship building a part of your strategy for achieving your goals?

In Chapter Eight, I show you a win-win approach to relationship building that can propel you far beyond traditional networking.

How many of your goals depend on the good will and support of others? If you are like me and the people I coach, most of your goals will have a relationship component. As simple as it sounds, often this relationship piece is the one that causes the most difficulty. That is because many people confuse relationship building with networking. If you have ever attended an event and spent the evening "wandering around marketing," with the vague idea that your ideal client must be here—somewhere—then you know what I mean. I am suggesting something entirely different. It is called NetWeaving.

Bob Littell first introduced Netweaving through his book, *The Heart and Art of NetWeaving*. In it, Bob gives us a framework for repositioning relationship building to a pay-it-forward model.

The expression "pay-it-forward" simply means that a person offers a debtor the option of paying the debt forward to a third person, instead of paying it back. Debt repayment can be monetary; it may be through good deeds. In this case, we're talking about good deeds. Benjamin Franklin was already using the pay-it-forward concept in business as early as 1784. Robert A. Heinlein wrote about it in his book, *Between Planets*, published in 1951. Pay-it-forward is nothing new, but its application to business building through NetWeaving may be brand new to you.

You already know that networking is primarily driven by the idea of building or adding to *your own* network. NetWeaving is based on the concept of helping *others* build or add to *their* network for *their* benefit. NetWeaving is simply connecting people, and positioning yourself as a resource to others. This is usually done on a totally gratuitous basis, with the expectation of "what goes around comes around." It's a win-win for the people who end up being connected, and it's a win for the NetWeaver who is the "matchmaker" or strategic connector.

The NetWeaver derives business benefits from NetWeaving, and there is the added "feel-good" benefit that only comes from helping others when one has no hidden agenda. Your role as NetWeaver can increase your chances of benefiting from the process in the long run. I call that "enlightened self-interest." As Bob Littell says, you may have been NetWeaving for much of your life, without having a name for it.

Bob goes on to explain that there are two key elements to NetWeaving. The first is learning to become a Strategic Connector *of* others. That is, putting people together in win-win relationships. The second is learning how to position yourself as a Strategic Resource *for* others, literally becoming the go-to person for making things happen. One added benefit is the immediate return on your investment, in the form of elevated and enhanced prestige and reputation. Being known as someone who wants more for others is a powerful magnet back to you.[16]

Now that you've got the basic idea, let's talk about how this works in practical terms. Let's say you want to help someone else achieve his or her goals. The process starts with information. In traditional networking, most conversations take place on a very superficial level. Talking about the weather, sports or the day's events doesn't take the conversation deep enough for you to make a real difference in the other person's results. With that said, you will have to lay a foundation for the questions you will ask to encourage the other person to open up to you in a business context. Before plunging into this new territory, you may want to briefly explain the NetWeaving concept to the other person.

For the purpose of this exercise, I want you to imagine you are a person seeking my assistance as a NetWeaver. The questions I will ask myself are designed to help me better understand your business and how I can help you. Listening to you will determine how I will proceed.

---

[16] Robert S. Littell, *The Heart and Art of NetWeaving,* 2003.

There are three questions I will ask myself:

1. **Is there someone I know who would benefit from knowing or meeting you?**
2. **Could you provide information and/or resources to someone else I know?**
3. **Have you impressed me so much that I need to get to know you better? If you continue to impress me with your exceptional quality, will I want to make you a part of my own Trusted Resource Network?**

Now I will begin our conversation:

- **First, tell me how you make your money.** I don't just mean what your business does, but how do you actually create revenue in your business?
- **What does a best prospect for you or your business look like?**
- **Tell me the story of how you landed your biggest or best client.** Your response will give me more insight into how you make a sale or create a client. Telling a story will help you more clearly articulate a process you may never have thought about, and your story will help me connect with you and retain the information.

Next, I will ask you:

- **What is your most burning problem, need, or opportunity in a business, family, or personal context where I might be able to help you?**
- **What is your Strategic Advantage?** As I am attempting to sell you to someone I know, or at least open a door for you, how do I describe you in terms that differentiate you from others doing the same or nearly the same thing?

Depending on the conversation, I might go on to ask:

- **What is the most valuable introduction or connection anyone ever made for you and why?**
- **What are the names of some people whom you would most like to meet?**
- **What are your key interests outside of work, and is there someone who would be an interesting contact for you in that area?**
- **What do you consider to be some of your most valuable information resources?**
- **How can I help you?**

As you become more adept at asking your own questions and facilitating your own connections, you will naturally advance from simply dabbling in conversation to becoming a world class NetWeaver.

Let's wrap up what we talked about in this chapter:

1. **Relationship building is an important strategy in achieving your goals.**
2. **Networking produces only limited results for advancing your business.**
3. **Paying-it-forward starts the magic of what goes around comes around.**
4. **Taking relationship building to a new level through NetWeaving will advance the goals of others *and* bring you both tangible and intangible rewards, including just plain feeling good about your role in someone else's success.** Your increased prestige and enhanced reputation are extra bonuses.

5. **Listening is as important as asking.** Going deep with others will enable you to benefit them better. Listening hard will help you make the best connections.

As Bob Littell reminds us, "Good things happen to people who make good things happen." You can learn more about NetWeaving at www.netweaving.com, where you can also purchase Bob's books, *Power NetWeaving: 10 Secrets to Successful Relationship Marketing*, which he co-wrote with Donna Fisher, and *The Heart and Art of NetWeaving*. Paying-it-forward himself, Bob donates 100 percent of the book purchase price to Junior Achievement and The Pay It Forward Foundation. He gives his book to any non-profit that wishes to use the book for fundraising purposes.

LEGAL & ETHICAL CONSIDERATIONS

Every lawyer wants to be a world class rainmaker. Every lawyer wants to bring in the long-term and loyal client that allows the firm to serve their needs for years to come. As you decide which prospects are worth the most of your precious time, remember that long relationships begin with a solid base. Do not expect that base to solidify in a single call or meeting. You must put in the time to develop the relationship. Great clients are born of great personal relationships.

Through Robin's process, you will eventually build a network of trusted advisors. Just as you will introduce clients and friends to these advisors, you will ask them to do the same for you. Keep in mind the following general principles and see Rule 7.3 for more detailed information:

- You may not employ or allow any person to perform any act that you are not permitted to perform.
- You may not pay a search firm or marketing firm a percentage of client fees.
- You may participate in lawyer referral services.

Building a network of trusted advisors is well within the ethical confines of the practice of law. I would argue that it is a basic tenet of the practice of law. Look again at Rule 1.1 Competence:

A lawyer shall provide competent representation to a client. Competent representation as used in this Rule means that a lawyer shall not handle a matter, which the lawyer knows or should know to be beyond the lawyer's level of competence *without associating another lawyer who the original lawyer reasonably believes to be competent to handle the matter in question.* Competence requires the legal knowledge, skill, thoroughness, and preparation reasonably necessary for the representation [emphasis added].

You must build a network of counsel who can assist with cases within and well outside the lawyer's area of expertise. Simply put, following Robin's advice in this chapter will make you more effective as a lawyer and broaden the types of cases you are able to handle.

Once you understand the benefits of building a referral network of lawyers, you need only take a short step to building a network of non-lawyers with whom you can support your clients. Through this support, you will refer clients to each other and without realizing it, you will build a referral network that will assist all of your contacts with client development.

Some clients will appreciate an opportunity to become a part of your referral network; others will not. A client must dictate the degree to which you safeguard the nature of your relationship. Even when your business obligation to the client is over, keep in mind that confidentiality extends beyond the end of the attorney/client relationship. Take the opportunity to ask the client if they wish to be included in your network and how you should explain your relationship with them when making introductions.

At its heart, business is conducted between people not companies. Therefore, you must build relationships with other people to build your business.

9

MASTER YOUR
E-COMMUNICATIONS

*As P. T. Barnum might have said, email is like
money—an excellent servant but
a terrible master.*

In Chapter Nine, we talk about how to turn email into the
excellent servant it was meant to be. Using specific strategies
for email will increase your effectiveness and decrease its
disruption to your time and attention.

First, let's talk about what email is and what it is not. Email
is not the same as hard copy, according to Dawn-Michelle
Baude, Ph.D. and author of *The Executive Guide to Email
Correspondence*. Dr. Baude explains the differences this
way[17]:

1. **Email is designed to move or transmit information
   as rapidly as possible, from the writer to the reader.**
   It usually produces immediate action, often in the form
   of another email. Hard copy, on the other hand, is

---

[17] Dawn-Michelle Baude, PhD., *The Executive Guide to E-Mail
Correspondence* (Franklin Lakes, NJ: The Career Press, Inc.)

designed for contemplation over time and does not necessarily move the reader to act. Email is a transaction; hard copy is a reflection.

2. **Unlike hard copy, email is more than rectangular.** It appears in a window, with clearly defined edges. These edges focus reading in a way that is very different from the way we read hard copy. The edge of a piece of paper is not so insistent. It's easier for the eye to lift, to wander, to reflect.

3. **Email is boxed-in with multiple frames that relentlessly focus the eye on the text.** Rigid borders confine the gaze and keep it on the words. The trapped-in quality of the text affects our expectation about the purpose and intent of reading. When we look at an email message, we expect to receive information, right away. We get frustrated when we don't get it.

Why is it important to see the email page differently from hard copy? If you understand how email information is seen and processed at a conscious and sub-conscious level, you can use that knowledge to create messages that are more likely to be read and acted upon. We'll talk more about this later in the chapter. Right now, let's shift attention to some of the basic rules of email courtesy.

First, we've got to be sure that people take us seriously when messages with our name in the header arrive in their inbox. The quickest way to brand yourself as someone who is silly and will fall for anything is to succumb to email chain letters and cutesy information that urges you to pass it along. Asking others to link to you on LinkedIn and/or other social media outlets can also be annoying. LinkedIn has become wildly popular. A listing there is considered imperative to one's professional career. If online networking services have proven to be a beneficial part of your practice-building strategy, then be sure to smooth the way with a brief email message in advance of your invitation to join. Be selective in your invitations, and make sure that you live up to your online profile. Keep in mind that your links are often public information, so use discretion. Do you want everyone to know who your clients are?

If your inbox is clogged, use spam protection to get rid of it. You can also direct email that isn't urgent, like newsletters and other subscriptions, to separate email accounts you can check later, at your leisure. You can then respond to your most important messages, without being slowed down by those that are not time-sensitive.

You wouldn't write a letter or a check and send it off without your signature, would you? An email without a signature isn't finished. It's also discourteous to the reader. Signatures are easy to set up so they will attach to every message, and they provide information about how you can be contacted. If you're not sure about how your email program handles signatures, your service provider should be able to help.

By the way, you may be surprised to learn that text messaging is rapidly replacing email. Email may never disappear entirely, but text messaging is the future and, if you haven't used it, you may want to find out how you can incorporate it into your communication strategies.

Now that you have thinned out your email inbox, stopped adding to what others may consider junk, and made it easy for people to contact you, let's talk about how to maximize your email impact.

Here are ten ways to make every message you send more effective:

1. **Make your message fast and easy for the reader.**

   - Map out your message so that the reader intuitively knows where to look for specific information.

   - The subject line is the first place the reader looks. Make the subject short and compelling, capturing the information like a newspaper headline would.

   - Include a signature line, as the reader will intuitively look for contact information there.

   - Make the message itself stand out with bulleted points that move the reader's eye where you want it to go.

2. **Write for skimming and scanning.**

   - Readers skim emails, giving different levels of attention to different parts.

   - They also scan, looking for specific information while ignoring the rest.

   - Set your emails up to help your reader do both.

3. **Use white space to speed up skimming and scanning.**

   - To skim and scan, the eyes need to move around the text, focusing in some places, resting in others.

   - A dense block of print discourages rapid eye movement.

   - Contrast speeds things up.

   - Alternating print with empty white space "gives the reader wings."

4. **Use white space to add meaning.**

   - White space is not empty. It's full of meaning.

   - White space tells the reader that there's a change in idea, a shift in the argument, an example on the way, a contrast coming, or an objection being raised.

- Readers use white space to navigate information for meaning.

5. **Make the first sentence count.**

- In business email, the first sentence of the text is the most important.

- Readers decide to read an email immediately or save it for later based on that first sentence.

6. **Begin with your conclusion, and then explain.**

- For replies, give your answer in the first sentence and explain your reasons below.

- To save time when making a request, tell the reader straight out what you want.

- For updates, summarize the situation in the first sentence and then detail it in the rest of the email.

- If you have a question, ask it right away. If the reader has asked you to reply, remind him or her of that at the start.

7. **Keep it simple to keep things moving.**

- Use headers and sub-titles to enhance skimming.

- Use short sentences and common vocabulary as much as possible.

- Keep your message length to screen size to eliminate scrolling.

- Use simple, straightforward language to get your message across right away.

- Use simple present and past tense.

- Use simple salutations. A first name followed by a comma is less formal, a name followed by a colon is more formal and signals something important is about to be said.

- Cut the email thread and start a new email (and subject line) when the length becomes cumbersome.

- Use the subject line to gain the reader's attention.

8. Build connection through your tone.

- Avoid using CAPITALS. The reader interprets them as SHOUTING.

- Avoid using punctuation such as exclamation marks ("!") when your message is intended to be formal!

9. Proof, then send.

- Always use Spell Check.

- Read to get a fresh perspective and to pick up typos and errors.

- Change the typeface to see your message with fresh eyes, or enlarge the type size.

- Print a hard copy.

- Read your message aloud to listen for errors.

10. Know when to call instead of emailing.

- Use the telephone to build or enhance your connection with the reader.

- Call to communicate how you feel.

- Call if you need to break bad news before you send the email.

- Call to reach resolution if emails have gone back and forth for a long period.

Email is an excellent servant, but it is you who must change in order to be its master. Set specific times of the day when you check your email. Use email with people who tend to be long-winded on the phone. Copy only those who need to know, and make friends with your "Delete" key. Be selective about to whom you give your email address, and treat your email just as you would hard copy: act on it, forward it, file it, or trash it.

For more on email dos and don'ts, sample texts for a variety of situations, and visual cues to give your messages more impact, pick up a copy *The Executive Guide to Email Correspondence* by Dawn-Michelle Baude, Ph.D.

LEGAL & ETHICAL CONSIDERATIONS

In reality, there is no way any lawyer can survive without communicating with clients via email. Clients prefer it, your staff need it to increase productivity and without it, you will be so far behind the time curve that you will never catch up! Learn to embrace email. When used properly, if it a force multiplier!

How can you control communication when you have ethical obligations to communicate with your clients? Is it ethical to turn off your email alerts? Is it ethical to have your staff review and respond to email? How can you control the 'email monster' that spews out emails all day, every day? Some of the best advice I ever received is to avoid checking your email when you first arrive in the morning. This will prevent one email from derailing your early morning plans. Finish the tasks *you scheduled* for the start of your day, and then check your email. The Rules require that you maintain open lines of communication with your clients. Rule 1.4 reads, in relevant part, "A lawyer shall . . . keep the client reasonably informed about the status of matters and shall promptly comply with reasonable requests for information." While you should take advantage of any technology that will assist you in your efforts to keep clients informed, you must manage the flow of your communication. As Comment 1B states, "'Prompt' communication with the client does not equate to 'instant' communication with the client and is sufficient if reasonable under the relevant circumstances."

Everything is relative, and there is not much that requires glancing at your PDA while having lunch with a client. Is this something you must do, or are you just being rude? Are you giving your client your undivided attention? Consider that only a few years ago, the concept of "instant communication" was

84

just that, a concept. Even in this era of high technology, the law still allows for documents to pass three days by standard mail.

What is reasonable communication under one set of circumstances may not pass muster in another scenario. Comment 2 to this Rule speaks to this concept. "The guiding principle is that the lawyer should fulfill reasonable client expectations for information consistent with the duty to act in the client's best interests and the client's overall requirements as to the character of representation." Some lawyers ask clients, "What is the best way to communicate?" Explore client preferences to help manage expectations and manage your time.

When using electronic communication, keep in mind the overriding principle of confidentiality. Rule 1.6 reads, in relevant part, "A lawyer shall maintain in confidence all information gained in the professional relationship with a client..." Therefore, make certain your clients understand the privacy limitations inherent in email communications. Ensure that clients are aware that staff will review or respond to email.

Emails can be intercepted or inadvertently forwarded to the wrong people. If you need to send an email that is private, you can purchase software to safeguard your client communications.

Consider the mindset of your new associate who just graduated from law school last spring, and college three years before that. They have always known email as a formal method of communication with Twitter, Facebook, or SMS being methods of communication. Having handled cases involving internet privacy and computer trespass, I have seen that most people, including lawyers, are ignorant of the degree to which electronic mail is neither private nor secure. You must discuss privacy with attorneys and explain the limitations of electronic mail. Further, if you recognize that electronic mail is the best way for you and your staff to communicate, you should provide a secure system to protect those communications.

As Robin states, email is a valuable tool. Use it wisely to facilitate communication with clients, but avoid the pitfalls!

10

ADD A PERSONAL TOUCH TO
EVERY INTERACTION

*A writer is a person for whom writing is more
difficult than it is for other people.*
– Thomas Mann

Technology may be changing the world, but the world still
runs on relationships. One very effective way to keep your own
world of business relationships running is by keeping in touch
through the simple act of writing a note.

In this chapter, we tackle the art of note writing and how
you can use this strategy to further advance your goals.

Note writing has been an important part of success
throughout history. When reviewing the achievers of the past,
the secret to who they really were is often contained in the
notes they wrote. The fact that these notes still exist today, that
they were saved, tells us how important notes can be.

If you are skeptical about how writing a note can make an
impact in today's ultra-high speed business world, here is what
Florence Isaacs says about it in her book, *Business Notes:
Writing Personal Notes That Build Professional Relationships.*
Isaacs says that, while exploring innovative applications for
writing notes, she found some surprising correlations between

note writing and success: the more impressive the job titles or the more successful the rainmakers, the more likely those individuals were to use note writing.[18] For instance, notes were used to woo new clients, cultivate customer loyalty, and motivate employees. She found that notes helped build and maintain a web of relationships both inside and outside the person's organization—a remarkable return on investment, wouldn't you say?

There's the time factor, of course. That's a given. But what is your real objection? Is it that the idea of writing is more frightening than the time it will take? I thought you might feel that way. German writer Thomas Mann captured the essence of why you don't need to worry about that. He said, "A writer is a person for whom writing is more difficult than it is for other people." Since it is more likely that you are the "other people," then writing should come a lot easier for you. Plus, you have another advantage. There are any number of books you can use to help you craft just the right message. A word of caution, though: while it is tempting to copy the messages you find in these books, your message must suit the situation and the relationship. A canned message defeats the purpose of note writing and may have the opposite effect.

On the reverse side, a short, plain-language canned message in the form of a hand-written note can sometimes produce surprising positive results. Florence Isaacs tells the story of a business owner who received a substantial and unexpected first-time order for his fairly common product from a customer he didn't know. Curious about how he got the business, he asked, "What made you choose us?" The customer replied that when he called and asked for information, everyone else just sent a brochure; but the owner's company sent a brochure and a hand-written note. The words that made the sale? The note

---

[18] Florence Isaacs, *Business Notes: Writing Personal Notes That Build Professional Relationships* (New York: Random House, 1998) 7.

simply said, "Dear So and So, Many thanks for your inquiry. I'm sure we can meet your needs. Sincerely, X." Closing with "sincerely" might be considered a cliché, but in this case the sentiment worked.[19]

Why did such a modest effort produce such rewarding results? In an age where everything changes at high speed, the personal touch is so rare that it stands out.

"But Robin, email is so much quicker and easier than taking the time to write something out by hand. Plus, I have to keep paper and stamps on hand and get the notes in the mail. Why isn't email a good option?" The answer is two-fold.

First, a hand-written note slows the whirl of business down long enough for you to say that this (issue, meeting, event, interview, sale) is important, and that this (client, interviewer, acquaintance) is important. Second, a hand-written note is tangible. Email is ephemeral. It comes in, is read and then disappears back into the ethers. Hand-written notes can be savored and revisited. They may even be posted for others to see. I know a real estate closing attorney who keeps a basket of thank-you notes she has received on a table where they can be easily seen as her clients pass by. This casual display sets an expectation that anyone who deals with her will have a positive experience.

Let's turn our attention to the situations that might lend themselves to a note, and develop an approach to note writing that will become easier and more common place.

Someone you have worked with wins an award. You spot an article that would be of interest to a client. Perhaps it's a client that you haven't heard from in quite some time, and you

---

[19] Isaacs, *Business Notes: Writing Personal Notes That Build Professional Relationships*, 33.

want to reconnect. These are just a few examples of events that might trigger a note. But what do you say? The secret to good note writing is finding your focus. Florence Isaacs suggests that there are five steps to focusing your efforts:[20]

1. **To whom are you writing?** The language, and even the stationery you use, will depend on the recipient. Who is this person and what is the relationship to you? What is the event or occasion this note is meant to recognize?

2. **How well do you know this person?** Writing to someone you just met is often more of a challenge than writing to someone you know well. It also determines whether your note will be more formal or casual.

3. **Why are you writing?** Your purpose will determine its style and content.

4. **How do you feel about the person or event that is at the heart of the note?** Your feelings are important. Expressing them well can make your note memorable.

5. **What do you want to convey?** Whether it's congratulations, gratitude, sympathy, encouragement, admiration, or something else, once you know what you want to express, your message will flow more easily. This is the time when you are most vulnerable to copying a message from one of the many note-writing resources; however, it is your voice and your personality that are important in conveying your message.

Isaacs says that there are five devices you can use in crafting your message. Consider using one or more of these in your note:[21]

---

[20] Isaacs, 18-20
[21] Ibid., 21-25.

1. **Make your message specific to the situation.** Include details that tie the reader back to the event or situation wherever you can. For example, if you are thanking someone for his help, then say what that help was. Instead of a generic, "Thank you for your help," say "Thank you for your help today at the meeting. Your participation made it a remarkable experience for everyone."

2. **Mention the person's hobbies and interests to help you make a connection.** Pay attention to clues the other person may give you, or by noticing what he has in his office. Books on sports or desktop items that may give you a hint. Notice what information you may pick up in casual conversation so that you can, when writing your note, mention her passion for gardening or spy thrillers. For example, if you are confirming that person's participation in a conference, you might say, "The conference is set for September 12. See you there. P.S. Hope the nine-hour flight gives you plenty of time to catch up on that new thriller you've been itching to read."

3. **Send clippings or other items of interest whenever you can.** I love this suggestion. It has so many possibilities and adds an extra dimension to the tangible benefits of the note. Some obvious clippings include articles on items of interest, like an article on wines and a note that references that. Even more powerful—an item you cut out of the local paper that announces your client's promotion. Send it along with a note across the page that says, "I know you will be running the place soon." How much more impact that message has! You'll find more ideas like that in Isaacs' book.

4. **Use quotes and statistics to underscore your message.** You don't have to rely solely on your own abilities to turn a phrase. Others may have captured the essence of

what you want to say better than you could. You still get credit for including their brilliance in your message. Google the word "quotations" and you will find dozens of quotation sites. Simply enter a topic you want to search and choose the one that best fits your needs.

5. **If you are stuck, consider using an all-purpose phrase.** Your notes need not always be original works of literary art. Sometimes a simple, "Thinking of you," or "Wishing you the best of everything," will communicate your feelings in the best light. Add enthusiasm, by starting a sentence with "How" as in "How thoughtful of you," or "How generous you are." The word "what" is also a great starter as in "What great news," or "What a great job you did on that brief."

No matter what the purpose of your note, pay attention to the details:

- **Use proper grammar, make sure notes are neat, and that every word is correctly spelled.** Notes with words crossed through look careless and rushed.

- **Write conversationally, avoiding stiff or stilted language that may appear insincere.**

- **Use humor sparingly and carefully.** What's funny to you may not be so to the person receiving your note.

- **Avoid using jargon, those words or terms that may mean something to you but nothing to your reader.**

Your time may be limited; but if you don't take enough time, your notes will imply that you are just writing the note to serve your own purposes; that the other person is not the center of your attention. If you won't take the time to do it right, then don't do it at all.

If you want more on note writing with sample texts for many common business situations, pick up a copy of Florence Isaacs' *Business Notes: Writing Personal Notes That Build Professional Relationships.*

LEGAL & ETHICAL CONSIDERATIONS

No one ever hired a law firm. Clients hire a lawyer. Even Mr. Marbury selected Charles Lee to represent his interests in Marbury v. Madison. *Before, during and after the representation, the attorney-client relationship is between two people. You must take the time to develop that relationship at every opportunity.*

Note writing is an excellent way to stay in touch and maintain a relationship. This is especially true when contacting past clients and other people with whom you have a relationship. Use caution, as your note could be perceived as unsolicited advertising, especially if you are sending the note to a stranger and seeking to promote your services. In those situations, you should refer to the Rules regarding advertising discussed in previous sections.

When speaking with associates about rainmaking, remember this is just a matter of creating relationships. They must learn to put themselves and your firm in the forefront of the potential client's mind. Do some research and find something in common with the prospective client. This exercise will assist your associates as they learn to find common ground with witnesses, current clients and other counsel. Robin's recommendations are about treating people with respect. This is the essence of our profession.

A POST SCRIPT FROM ROBIN ON WORLD CLASS RAINMAKING

What we think, or what we know, or what we believe is, in the end, of little consequence. The only consequence is what we do.
– John Ruskin

If you are serious about becoming a world class rainmaker, then applying the strategies and tactics outlined in this book will propel you towards your goals.

- **Take time to plan.** As I talked about in Chapter One, the results you are working towards start with setting realistic goals.
- **Change your mind about time.** Compressing the time you have to do what needs to be done increases the urgency of every action you take. Taking those actions every day produces an inevitable good outcome.
- **Increase your productivity** to increase the output of what really matters by delegating those tasks that will benefit both you and those whose careers will be enhanced by being asked to raise their own bar.
- **Commit to tackling your worst jobs first**, then be sure you do them first on a consistent basis.
- **Manage the time you spend in meetings**.
- **Add a sabbatical to your annual plans** to refresh and renew yourself for achieving your goals.
- **Recognize those that contribute to the firm's success** by giving them a meaningful role to play that goes beyond a mere thank-you.

- **Maximize your new and old relationships** by introducing new networking strategies that include learning about and helping others to achieve their goals.
- **Leverage email and other electronic communication** to build connection more quickly and effortlessly.
- **Reintroduce the sincere and personal handwritten note** to your relationship building protocols.

Adopting the strategies and tactics laid out in *The World Class Rainmaker: Raising the Bar in Your Law Practice* will help you build a foundation for achieving your goals. If you would like to take yourself and your firm even higher, consider inviting me to coach you and/or your team. Working together we will focus on how to 1) produce a steady stream of new clients for your practice, 2) increase revenue from existing clients and 3) maximize the return from non-billable business development time while still achieving your billable time goals.

SOME WORDS OF ENCOURAGEMENT FROM LANCE FOR YOUNG LAWYERS ON THE PARTNER TRACK

Partner: an owner of part of a company, usually a company he or she works in, who *shares both the financial risks and the profits* of the business.[22] (emphasis added)

Making partner is a process. Most young lawyers want to know the time required to partnership at the outset believing that partnership is based upon tenure with the firm or the number of hours worked in a year. However, the path to partnership involves a great more than the number of days you work with the firm or a tally of hours. The period between the day you start and the day you receive an offer of partnership, should be a long interview process. That interview process should involve two-way communication and a process that requires a great deal of investigation on your part.

You should work hard every day at your job, and I hope that you will enjoy and learn to love the practice of law. However, you should keep your eyes open at all times while working toward partnership. Look at the senior members of the firm. Do they enjoy the practice of law? Do they take time for themselves and their families? Do they have rewarding personal lives? More importantly, do they have a book of business that consists of loyal clients or do they rely upon the firm's reputation to bring in clients?

Becoming a partner means learning and adapting to the way business is conducted in the firm. Simply put, in ten or twenty

---

[22] *Encarta English Dictionary*

years, is this the life you want to have as a partner? Do you want more out of the balance of life and work than has been attained by those who came before you? You may decide that you are not excited about the prospect of becoming partner at a particular firm because the price of partnership is too high.

With regard to the rainmaking requirements to make partnership, be very careful if there are none. On the other hand, a healthy partnership track will require you to build a book of business of your own and true mentors will teach you how to do so. There are so many attorneys, including partners, who are forced to leave firms every year because their work "dried up."

This happened many times in the Atlanta and other markets following the economic downfall that began in earnest in 2008. Some of my friends found themselves unemployed when the power and reputation of the firm was not enough to weather the economic downturn and provide work for every practice group. Let me be clear, these people were employed with some of the largest, most prestigious firms in Atlanta. Associates and partners alike were cut from the payroll when a group of clients stopped calling and the current projects reached completion.

There is no insurance for job security in the legal profession. There is no tenure either. Partnership is no longer a guarantee of employment or an income in our profession. No firm is immune from cuts and no lawyer, irrespective of partnership status, is immune from receiving walking papers.

So, once you decide that you are in the right firm and you want to make partner, you must build job security and protection for yourself. You cannot rely upon anyone or any firm to insure your career and livelihood. There is only one path to a long, successful career in the law filled with prosperity and personal satisfaction. You must begin now to build your own book of business and work to manage your time to maintain a balance between your personal and professional life.

Finally, you must recognize that you are building your personal career, not the career of the other lawyers around you or the partner with whom you work. If you want to learn more about an area of law but the firm will not approve a CLE class outside your practice area, pay for the class yourself and take vacation time to attend. It is a small price to pay for security and balance in your career and your life. This includes paying out of your own pocket, if necessary, to hire Robin Hensley to teach you how to build your own book of business.

Read this book, practice the principles outlined herein and you will find that the path to a productive and rewarding partnership is much shorter when you have your own clients and book of business to offer the firm.

BIBLIOGRAPHY

"Successful Delegation: Using the Power of Other People's Help," *MindTools*,
http://www.mindtools.com/pages/article/newLDR_98.htm
1999.

Baude, Dawn-Michelle, PhD. *The Executive Guide To E-Mail Correspondence: Including Model Letters for Every Situation.* Franklin Lakes, NJ: The Career Press, Inc., 2006.
Career," Monster.com.

Encarta English Dictionary. New York: St. Martin's Press,
global/en/meetingsinamerica/uswhitepaper.php

Harvard Business Communication: A Newsletter From Harvard Business School "10 Commandments of Meeting," November 1, 1999.
http://career-advice.monster.com/in-the-office/work-life-balance/take-a-sabbatical-without-derailing/article.aspx
https://e-meetings.verizonbusiness.com/

International Association of Administrative Professionals (IAAP), "When did Administrative Professionals Week begin?" http://www.iaap-hq.org/events/apw/faq

Isaacs, Florence. *Business Notes: Writing Personal Notes That Build Professional Relationships.* New York: Random House, 1998.

LeVan, Gerald. *Lawyers Lives Out of Control: A Quality of Life Handbook.* LeVan Co, 1993.

Littell, Robert S. *The Heart and Art of NetWeaving,* 2003.
Mass: Merriam-Webster, 2003.

Merriam-Webster's Collegiate Dictionary 11th ed. Springfield,
Moran, Brian and Lennington, Michael. *Periodization: 12*
Rossheim, Josh. "Take a Sabbatical Without Derailing Your
Sahadi, Jeanne. "The World's Best Perk", CNNMoney, June 13, 2006.
http://money.cnn.com/2006/06/13/commentary/everyday/sahadi/index.htm

State Bar of Georgia, http://www.gabar.org/barrules/

Tracy, Brian. *Eat That Frog! 21 Great Ways to Stop Procrastinating and Get More Done in Less Time.* San Francisco: Berrett-Koehler Publishers, Inc., 2007.

Verizon Conferencing White Paper, "Meetings in America, A study of trends, costs and attitudes toward business travel, teleconferencing, and their impact on productivity. Greenwhich, CT: INFOCOMM, 1998.

Weeks to Breakthrough. Holt, MI: Strategic Breakthroughs, 2003.

ABOUT ROBIN HENSLEY

THE BUSINESS DEVELOPMENT COACH
FOR WORLD CLASS RAINMAKERS
PRESIDENT, RAISING THE BAR

Robin Hensley, The Business Development Coach for World Class Rainmakers, is founder and president of Raising the Bar. Ms. Hensley specializes in coaching managing partners, team leaders, super rainmakers, and other key law and accounting firm profitability leaders. She is author of the book, *Raising the Bar: Legendary Rainmakers Share Their Business Development Secrets* as well as numerous eBooks, articles, and publications.

Ms. Hensley held business development and marketing positions with the Atlanta law firms Kilpatrick Townsend & Stockton LLP and Swift, Currie, McGhee & Hiers, LLP and she was also a CPA with Ernst & Young. She currently serves on the board of directors of Superior Uniform Group, listed on NASDAQ, where she has chaired the audit committee for more than ten years. She served on the board of directors of Northside Hospital for ten years. She has been honored to serve on The Atlanta Legal Aid Society Advisory Board and is an alumna of Leadership Atlanta.

As a business development coach, Ms. Hensley's work has been featured in numerous publications, including *Managing Partner Magazine*, *Journal of Accountancy*, *National Law Review*, *Corporate Board Magazine*, the *Atlanta Business Chronicle*, *Atlanta Journal-Constitution* and *Daily Report*.

Learn more about Robin and her practice at www.raisingthebar.com.

ABOUT LANCE LORUSSO

PRINCIPAL ATTORNEY AND OWNER
LORUSSO LAW FIRM

Lance LoRusso is principal attorney and owner of the LoRusso Law Firm, with an extensive background in law enforcement. Lance's years of experience in criminal and civil litigation allow him to advocate for his clients to prevent, respond to, and pursue litigation.

The focus of his practice is medical malpractice defense, general liability defense, healthcare law, representation of professionals before licensing boards, and catastrophic personal injury and wrongful death cases on behalf of injured parties and their families. His representation of healthcare systems, professional organizations and corporate clients has provided a broad range of expertise.

Lance graduated *cum laude* from the Georgia State University College of Law. He holds a Master of Public Administration degree from Kennesaw State University, and a Bachelor of Arts in Educational Studies from Emory University.

As a former police officer, Lance is honored to serve as General Counsel to the Georgia Fraternal Order of Police. He also responds to critical incidents on behalf of law enforcement officers, advocating for them in professionally and personally stressful situations. Lance continues to serve the community as an instructor for police academies throughout the state.

Lance writes professional journal and newsletter articles and speaks to business owners, healthcare professionals, and risk managers. His articles appear in lawenforcementtoday.com, officerresource.com, SWAT magazine, and other publications.

He has served as an expert for interviews with media such as CNN, *Atlanta Journal-Constitution, Marietta Daily Journal, Daily Report, Inside Cobb*, all Atlanta TV stations, and numerous radio stations.

As part of his efforts to give back to the community, Lance serves as member of the board of directors for Easter Seals of North Georgia and Hunting for Heroes (www.huntingforheroes.org), a non-profit that provides peer counseling and support for law enforcement officers who are severely injured in the line of duty.

Learn more about Lance and his practice at www.lorussolawfirm.com and through his blog, www.bluelinelawyer.com. You can find him on LinkedIn, Facebook, and Twitter. He will release a book in 2012 on officer involved shootings.

FOR MORE INFORMATION

For additional copies of *The World Class Rainmaker: Raising the Bar in Your Law Practice,* information about coaching services and programs, and/or to subscribe to Raising the Bar's free on-line business development information, please visit our website, write, or email:

Robin Hensley
President, Raising the Bar
999 Peachtree Street N. E.
Suite 1234
Atlanta, GA 30309-4484
404-815-4110
404-601-7494 (f)
www.raisingthebar.com / info@raisingthebar.com
www.theraisingthebarblog.com
www.linkedin.com/in/robinhensley

Lance LoRusso
Principal Attorney and Owner
LoRusso Law Firm
1827 Powers Ferry Road SE
Building 8 Suite 200
Atlanta, GA 30339
770-644-2378
770-644-2379 (f)
lance@lorussolawfirm.com
www.lorussolawfirm.com
www.bluelinelawyer.com